An Uncrowded Place

The delights and dilemmas of life Up North
and a young man's search for home

BOB BUTZ

HURON
RIVER
PRESS

10 9 8 7 6 5 4 3 2

ISBN: 978-1-932399-21-9

Huron River Press
08½ South State Street
Suite 30
HURON Ann Arbor, MI 48104
RIVER
PRESS www.huronriverpress.com

Printed in the United States of America.

LIBRARY OF CONGRESS CATALOGING-IN-PUBLICATION DATA

Butz, Bob, 1971-
  An uncrowded place : the delights and dilemmas of life up north and a young man's search for home : a book by Bob Butz.
     p. cm.
  Includes bibliographical references.
  ISBN 1-932399-21-6
  1. Butz, Bob, 1971- 2. Life change events--Michigan. 3. Small cities--Michigan. 4. Mountain life--Michigan. 5. Michigan--Biography. I.
     Title.
       CT275.B8383A3 2008
       977.4'043--dc22
                                        2008034252

For Jeff Smith

Acknowledgments

Thanks to Jeff Smith, the editor of *TRAVERSE: Northern Michigan's Magazine*. Over a decade ago, I sent him a little essay—"Dream Fish, Night Fish"—hoping he might consider publishing it as a contribution to a regular feature in the magazine called "Up in Michigan."

Jeff (to whom this book is also dedicated)—along with then managing editor Cara McDonald (now the Deputy Editor for Denver-based *5280* and still one of the most creative and insightful magazine editors I know)—liked that first essay enough that they opened the door for what has become a long and wonderful collaboration.

At the time, I didn't know I was writing a book. Those early essays and vignettes, about half of which are included here, were always fun (and sometimes cathartic) to write. But after each was finished, I treated the pages as one might a snapshot or a letter from a faraway friend. I saved them without really knowing why. A couple of years ago, I found that folder full of writings and, for fun, sat down to look over what was inside.

Piece by piece, it didn't take long for me to see a story beginning to form. So I wrote and rewrote, reorganized and, finally, gave an early draft of what I thought was a book with some pretty good unity to a writer friend—Hillary Porter—who offered helpful editorial and creative advice. Heather Shaw, Editor-in-Chief of *Foreword Magazine*, was the one who suggested I send the manuscript to Huron River Press. I am thankful to Heather for the advice and her friendship over the years. And, of course, I'm grateful to the owners of Huron River Press, Steve and Shira Klein, for the keen interest and excitement they showed in the project the first time we met face-to-face at Art's Tavern in Glen Arbor. They ordered first—the whitefish burger with Tater Tots™—and, as far as I was concerned, it was pretty much a done deal after that. If you're not from this little corner of northern Michigan, maybe by the end of this book you'll understand.

Table of Contents

Up North

L et's take a moment to orient ourselves. The place we're headed is north. Just follow the ducks and skeins of geese heading home. Or easier still, simply pile into something with four-wheel drive (you'll need it if you plan on wintering here) and follow the highway signs—the odd numbered ones—up into the tall timbered hills and deep piney forests rippling up from the plow fields; the flat, farm country lowlands; cities; and sprawling suburbs down below. Go until the hardtop ends in the territory near or beyond the 45th parallel, just this side of Canada.

The question at hand is not how to find your way north, but rather how to know when you've finally arrived.

Like the Deep South, it's a region within itself that's hard to pinpoint on a map. Latitude is our Mason-Dixon Line, but it's an arbitrary boundary. Better to watch for those hand-painted road signs advertising apple cider and maple syrup for sale. BEEF JERKY, SMOKED WHITEFISH, and U-PICK BLUEBERRIES. GOOD LUCK DEER HUNTERS. Look for pine and cedars trees, aspen and white birch. Here REAL MEN LOVE JESUS and the ravens in the sky outnumber the crows.

I'm writing from up in Michigan, my little corner of the North, home to Paul Bunyan and Babe the blue ox, Hemingway's Nick

Adams, Longfellow's Hiawatha, and the big lake called Gitche-
gumee. Here all the rivers and streams run cold. Everybody owns a
trout rod, a pair of skis or snowshoes, and at least one canoe. It's a
country located in the Upper Midwest, a place of mystery and myth
that is shaped, fittingly I think, like the back of your left hand.

In fact, if you're ever up this way and stop to ask directions, the
folks up here are liable to show you where you're going by drawing
it out on the back of their hand. If you've always lived here, it
probably doesn't seem like such an odd thing. But I'm from another
place so it just strikes me as kind of quaint how whenever anybody
wants to tell me where they're from, or where they're going, they
hold up their left hand and point to a spot on it.

There's an old saying about being able to tell most everything
about a person by looking at their hands; that's as true in Michigan,
maybe more so, than anywhere else. I'm learning that there's
something comforting in that: being able to find your place in this
world through something as simple as looking at your hands.

Traverse City.

It's exactly on the end of your pinkie.

Lost and Found

When it comes to discerning my right from left, I'm afflicted by a condition that could be called "directional dyslexia." It's hell on anyone who asks me for directions, and likewise when I'm taking them. In any event, my advice is to stand clear.

You see, to keep straight both incoming or outgoing information, I tend to talk with my hands. Think of it as frenzied sign language for the directionally challenged. *Stop sign turn left. Blinker light turn right.* When I really get going, such crazed chopping at the air has been likened by at least one friend to witnessing a scene reenacted from a Jackie Chan film.

Unless I go through these convulsions, I'll think *turn left* but say *turn right.* It's akin to a similar difficulty I have of knowing where in the alphabet a letter falls only after I've run through the entire sequence in my head. I'm talking about the A-B-C song children learn in elementary school. It's a definite pain when looking up a name in the phone book or checking a word in the dictionary.

The point is, I get "turned around" a lot.

It would be wrong to say I get "lost." Getting lost is what happens to a couple of hapless deer hunters every autumn. The criteria include one uncomfortable night spent outdoors and an organized search effort that lands your embarrassing predicament a spot on the local news. That's *really* lost.

When you're merely turned around, you get to feel helpless and stupid without alerting several public agencies and members of the press. And that's a good thing. Good, because I think to "go missing" for a while—however embarrassing—is to come back a touch enlightened, too.

3

I think there is something valuable in not always knowing exactly where you're going. People don't allow themselves to lose their direction very often, no more than we ever let ourselves be truly thirsty, hungry, or cold.

Used to be I considered myself something of a navigation wizard. My internal compass felt in cosmic tune. Chalk it up to youth (young people always act as if they know where they are headed even when they haven't a clue) and the fact that it's just plain impossible to get lost when you rarely stray from familiar ground.

Where I'm from, Pennsylvania, the foothills of the Appalachians, the mountains and valleys lend themselves to carefree overland travel. I used to know some old-timers back home who went their whole life without ever needing a compass.

Not so in northern Michigan, where the swamps are dark and tangled; where one cedar, aspen, or birch tree looks the same as the rest; and where the hills pitch and roll with the whimsy of the sea. It's as true here as anywhere that all streams flow downhill, and all rivers eventually lead to town. But up here, the water takes a circuitous route, lazy and meandering, and certainly in no hurry to get home.

If you've never circled back on your own tracks or passed the same landmark two, maybe three, times all while being convinced the line you took was straight, you can easily conjure that feeling of profound disbelief; when your instincts first fail you, it can be almost palpable. All of a sudden, you're not as smart as you think you are.

It's not so much the losing of one's path that I find so wonderful. It's in finding your way back again. It's about walking blind, perhaps in the grip of semi-panic at the prospect of spending the night in the woods and then taking that step and finally realizing where you are.

That's when the enlightenment comes in. I wonder what would it feel like to be lost if we didn't have anything or anyone to be lost to? It must be a little like dying and nobody noticing that we're gone. If you look at it that way, that's when you realize the beauty of being lost is being found and that being lost would mean nothing if we didn't have a way or a place to call home.

An Ax to Grind

Of all the outlandish objects and overpriced toys I desired as a child, I can barely recall any of them, save for my boyhood want for a double-bitted ax.

Admittedly, I was a kooky kid. So my mother was used to such odd requests. Except for a brief stint of wanting to be a professional bass fisherman, while other kids in the neighborhood were daydreaming of baseball diamonds and football fields, I was plotting to one day disappear into the wilderness and become a mountain man.

The trappings of such a life included a good ax. Unfortunately, I was not a farm kid anymore. We lived in an apartment complex after the divorce, so I might as well have asked for a .50 caliber Hawken gun.

A Michigan double-bit—so named by the lumbermen of the northwoods who, during the timber boom of 1850, accounted for timber sales a billion dollars greater than profits realized in the California Gold Rush—was the kind of ax you could build a log cabin with or fend off a grizzly bear.

With a good ax, you could build a home.

Even under the circumstances, mine was not an underprivileged childhood. But such a request was over the top. I never got my ax. Being all of eight years old at the time, no doubt my mother feared I would run amok and girdle every tree in that neighborhood, a place I wholly and utterly despised.

I got by with a hatchet picked up at a nearby construction site. In the swamp, I fashioned a half lean-to, half pit-cabin framed of thorny black locust and thatched with pine boughs. The plans for the shelter—minus the plywood floors and blue tarp walls—came from an issue of *Outdoor Life*. I had a stack of them stashed here, along with a small cooler filled with hot dogs and soda—a growing pile of illegal contraband, whatever I could pilfer from a nearby convenience store.

I had some issues, but this was my place. A tiny creek, chock-full of crayfish and red darters and water snakes, its muddy banks trampled with raccoon tracks, cut through the swamp right outside my door. One afternoon while roasting hotdogs shoplifted from the corner convenience store, I looked up from the fire to see a tiny red buck in full velvet staring at me from the other side.

The place was eventually happened upon by neighborhood kids and destroyed. My hatchet and other possibles vanished. I used to wonder, mournfully, when it was that things started going so haywire for me. In spite of everything that brought me here, it always goes back to this: coming upon my ransacked hideout—my salvation—and collapsing in the dirt at the realization that most of what I cared for was gone.

Over the years, I gradually opened myself up to cities, towns, and people, which I now love far too much to ever live away from. When I finally settled down and moved to northern Michigan, it occurred to me one day to go looking for the kind of ax I had never been allowed.

Finding such an ax, even in the land of its namesake, wasn't as simple as laying out the money for one. A Michigan double-bit—the kind of ax Paul Bunyan used to carry—has a three-foot handle and a three-pound head. One side is ground thin for felling trees, the other thicker for camp chores.

I struck out at the lumberyard. No go at Sears and no dice at the hardware store down the road.

The clerk at the hardware store was a hunched-over old man

with big, white teeth. The gold nametag on his shirt said "Milton." Right away, Milton tried to sell me a maul. When I told him it was for cutting down trees, not chopping up firewood, he looked at me like I was pulling his leg or something, shook his head, then (speaking very slowly in what can best be described as Mister Rogers-speak) told me that people don't use axes to cut down trees anymore.

He opened this big book on the counter that had pictures of tools in it. Moving his finger down over the pages, he asked me again what kind of ax I wanted, and what I wanted it for. I told him I was a trapper and that maybe I would use it to cut through the ice when checking my beaver sets. He looked up at me with his crooked digit on the middle of the page, all bent over and smiling as if he was about to tell me some big joke.

"So what are you then? A lumberjack or a mountain man?" he said.

I told him that maybe I'd use it to cut down a tree to make a bow.

"Jee-zus," he said, "now yer an Indian." With that, he turned the book on the counter so I could see the pictures of the different axes, pointing to the one that said, Michigan double-bit: $25.95.

Rarely has happiness come so cheap.

The Land Where Wandering Lovers Go

Last evening over drinks and a little gettin'-to-know-ya session with the new neighbors, the conversation eventually got around to how everybody ended up here. It has been my experience that to actually meet anyone from northern Michigan is quite rare, especially among thirty-something couples who all seem to have moved here from Detroit, Saginaw, and Flint. Everyone seems to have the same sand-castle memories of vacations at the beach or that ubiquitous "cottage on the lake." The goodness of this place, the pride and tacit understanding of the financial sacrifice anyone of meager means makes when trying to call the country home always plays big in the retelling. As does the romance, this idea of having finally arrived together in this childhood notion of heaven, and making it—a life—here, together.

They told their story and then Nancy told ours and, I guess, some time has passed since I'd really considered how much the northern magic worked on us, too.

I've always thought of myself as the kind of person who could be happy most anywhere and, it bears mentioning, alone. After college, to make ends meet, I clerked part time at this bait and tackle shop where my primary responsibility was packing worms— nightcrawlers mostly, a baker's dozen in every Styrofoam cup, sold to the constant parade of fishermen in and out the ding-dong door. Honest work, but for once I wanted a job I could be proud of, like Nancy, who already had a *real job*, complete with her very own business cards, travel, and expense accounts.

Lucky for me, she had a good sense of humor, too, and enough of an artsy bent to find charming the whole struggling-writer thing. We had one evening together, a dinner date, set up by her sister, the wife of my boss at the shop. Then I was scheduled to leave town. She and I both knew it. I even pointed out on the map where I was headed: north toward the border, almost to Canada.

"Call me when you get settled *down* there," she said. Neither of us recognized at the time that we shared a lot more than just a quirky dysfunction with direction.

I found northern Michigan on the leading edge of the worst winter in decades. Sixty degrees below zero with the wind, one night was so cold you could throw a cup of water into the air and the little droplets would freeze and make a shattering noise when they hit the ground. Snow blew into that drafty little cabin under the front door and down the rusted chimney pipe of the pot-bellied woodstove my no-good landlord never would get around to fixing. I curled in my sleeping bag on the hard wood floor, the red numbers of the digital alarm clock my only illumination. Listening to my wristwatch ticking, a torturous noise amplified by the blackened emptiness of that tiny room, I started thinking about Nancy and how maybe we could salvage a laugh out of this.

I got her machine and almost hung up before leaving this silly rambling message:

"The snow here is just incredible," I said (like it was a good thing)…"And the job's great" (which it wasn't)…"Anyway, I just found your number. Unpacking, you know. And well, ah, gotta get back to it…"

By now the snow spitting from the woodstove was wisping around my slippers. A small drift had formed on the carpet inside the door.

"Oh hell," I said, pushing the sock hat back off my brow, "I'm lying. Can you give me a call? I'd really like to talk to you."

Now back at the neighbors'…sharing what was clearly a moment of unmanly vulnerability always plays well with the other wives. It's one of the romantic hooks of the story. Likewise, the every-week letters I began sending and every-day calls that followed. But the real biggie, the one that never fails to get even me, is that we only had something like eighteen days together. There was only that surprise trip to see her on Christmas Eve that first year and a handful of winter weekends in between when Nancy, traveling cross-country for business, would take side trips here before either of us realized that whatever you called what we were doing might be worth more of an honest go.

The first time she visited was during a freakish Halloween blizzard. I picked her up at the airport and we went sledding all the while with me thinking that if icy winds and gusting snow in October weren't enough to scare her away, surely the end would be soon in coming when we got back to my place and she saw how little my poverty had changed since my worm-packing days.

Home was a cold, empty cave I tried to warn her about, "You don't understand. I have five-gallon buckets for chairs." Paper plates and plastic spoons—throwaway things that would have struck an ordinary woman as hopelessly dead-end—Nancy will recall today as cozy and romantic.

I'd never been in love before, not like that. It fills me up in such a way that I can't help but think this is how every true love should play out. For me, it happened like this—starting out with nothing, striking out into unknown territory, searching for the perfect place to call my own.

One day I woke up lying on an air mattress in the middle of a cold floor, inside a house with no furniture. Outside it was snowing and inside I could see my breath. But I wasn't cold anymore. I looked around the room and saw her things—an open suitcase and her clothes draped on one of my cheap plastic patio chairs. The two of us lay there wrapped in a quilt, her and me and me and her. I looked outside, through the pane of glass, to see that the snow had stopped falling and realized at that instant that this tiny place in the world was special, not on account of geography alone, but because it suddenly belonged to both of us now.

Wild Hair

A great personal misgiving of mine is the fact that I don't have the face for growing a beard. I don't have the follicles for it, or better said, I simply lack complete coverage. What I can grow is just plain spotty, mangy looking, and according to my wife, "utterly gross." A hard truth, one that runs contrary to the image I'd like to project—that of a rugged, take-it-on-the-chin outdoorsman.

A woodsman should wear a beard, especially in winter, the time I most lament my hairless jowls. Long before the snow clouds blow over the big water out from the north, I've pulled from the closet and readied my cold-weather digs: my green Mackinaw Cruiser, red Union suit, and Filson bibs. I swap everything flannel for everything wool.

Admittedly, my get-up—down to the tin cup full of coffee on the dash of the pickup—is overcompensation for an overt flaw in my outdoorsy persona. Though it would be quite a stretch for me to claim knowledge of every plant in the woods, every bird song and wildflower, I would at least like to look the part.

My wife likes the appearance of a well-kept beard, which only furthers the injustice. A beard suggests courage, strength, imagination, and resourcefulness. Good providers wear beards. Just think of the greatest giver of all, Santa Claus. Furthermore, what is more fatherly than a man with a beard? I remember from my schoolbooks that Shakespeare himself had plenty to say about "beardless boys." It makes me wonder what our little ones will think come autumn, when all the other fathers, in getting ready for deer camp, begin sporting some scruff while their daddy's face remains as bald as the T.V. screen.

Even up here in the northwoods, sporting a whiskered mug is about as in-vogue as a cheek-full of chewing tobacco. Still, I say, Jimmy Buffett can have my pencil-thin mustache. Just as I take the occasional plug of chew, I would wear a beard despite the social implications.

What better picture of a winter woodsman can one muster than that of an old grizzled hunter dressed in plaid—icicles clinging to his mustache and a hoarfrost covering his graying beard—sitting on a stump, smoking a pipe, and contemplating the cold?

For me, it would be a matter of both form and function. A little stubble would buffer my face from alder whips when ducking through the autumn bird cover hot after the dog. Come winter, how better to ward off that pesky chill at neckline than with a few months' growth?

A beard offers a look both woodsy and artsy. Just consider one bearded fellow named Hemingway. Back when I was in college trying to write like Hemingway, I kept an old newspaper photo of him thumbtacked to the bookshelf over my desk. The image showed the author as an old man, complete white facial fittings and a wry smile that suggested he still had a wild hair. In no other photos did he appear quite as *writerly*.

All the greatest heroes wore beards. It's a tradition one can trace back to the time of Odysseus. Young men learn this even today, though the circumstances are typically less than virtuous. My experience was that the baby face only got the girl in the movies, while the hero in college was the one whose facial hair helped to consistently dupe the party store clerk to secure for the rest of us ample quantities of illegal smokes and beer.

Vexed by a bit of trouble the other day, I caught myself deep in thought, stroking my chin and wishing for whiskers that weren't there. A beard would make the answers to tough questions elementary... I'm sure of it. Every great thinker who has ever pondered the infinite seems to have worn a beard.

It's a silly notion, I admit, but I think a beard speaks of all things good. The best reason of all, at least to my way of thinking, is how a beard conjures images and feelings of wildness, the wildness left in a man and perhaps in us all.

A Hunting Cabin

Someday I'll have a hunting cabin. I haven't decided exactly where. About the only thing I am sure of is that it will be north of wherever I happen to be living at the time. North because I like the feeling the word conjures up. I like the idea of *headin'* north (it isn't a direction you merely *go*). I want to be able to ditch work at 5:00 sharp and have my truck waiting outside all gassed up, packed, and ready to go. Headin' Up North! Driving back roads half the night with the windows down, nothing but cold country air whipping through the open cab, and not stopping until I get there—not ever slowing down, except, of course, for the occasional deer standing in the middle of the road.

It will be a tiny log cabin, hemmed in by snow, tucked away under the heavy white boughs of the spruce and cedar trees. A long lane will wind its way back through the woods for a mile or so, then over a narrow wooden bridge under which a tiny stream will flow. It'll become my habit to stop there to look for trout fining in the shallows and to hear the sound of the water that lets me know I've arrived.

When I pull up in the drive in the middle of that cold winter night, the headlights will pan over all the firewood I started cutting back in summer. Cords and cords of tightly stacked, glorious wood!

It will be another one of my rituals, to start chopping wood in August, after a morning of fishing on the creek or out back on the quiet lily pad lake. On those days, swinging my trusty double-bitted ax will feel so good that no doubt I'll cut up more firewood than I'll need. But on those cold nights in winter, it'll feel satisfying to see it all there—great walls of wood—stacked up outside between the trees.

I'll sit in the cab with the engine idling, looking things over, then double-check the pockets of my heavy wool Mackinaw for matches and the key to the padlock on the door. Pulling the flashlight out from under the seat, I'll step outside and take a deep breath of the cold night air. The moon will be shining full, nearly as bright as the sun. And the stars—there will be so many stars.

Once on the porch, I'll stomp the snow off my boots and inside find the lantern on top of the stove. With the fire going, I'll get my tin cup and the bottle down from the sill and pour myself a little whiskey. I'll drink it in front of the big window where, looking down over the tops of the trees, I'll see the lake frozen and snow covered. White as far as the eye can see.

I'll remember my gear out in the truck, but will take my time getting it. Between each trip, I'll stand a moment by the fire to get warm. Finally, when everything is inside, I'll hang my bow from the big deer antlers on the wall—for luck. Then I'll throw another log on the fire, sit again, and look at each arrow in my quiver, thumbing the edge of the broadheads, and touching each up with a file whether they need it or not.

In the morning it will be snowing, snow piled up as high as the railing on the porch when I step outside. I'll take the snowshoes down from the wall and place them beside the door with my daypack, arrows, and bow. Then I'll stoke the fire, pour a cup of coffee, and sit in my chair by the window. I'll probably think about the quiet of the place, the stillness. I'm a young man now, so no doubt I'll relish the solitude. But when I'm old…if I'm old…I think I'd rather share this place, and a morning such as this, with someone else.

I'm not talking about a woman, though I suppose it would be

nice to look around and see the one I dearly love still asleep under the covers. I'm talking about a someday-child—the son or daughter Nancy and I talk of having, maybe, one day—a giddy, slaphappy young hunter who just can't wait to get out the door to go hunting.

I'll don't think I'll ever quit hunting, but I suspect someday the urge to kill game will not grip me as it does now. Surely the warmth of the cabin will feel better every season, and I will find it harder and harder to trek out into the cold. The day might even come when I'll need someone there to hurry me along. If that day ever arrives, I hope there is someone to pass it all down to; I hope there is a place for that little one to go.

Mining for Morels

It's an understatement to say, "I'm just *not very good* at finding morels." A friend's eight-year-old son, already an accomplished mushroom finder, summed up it best last year. Staring mournfully into my empty pail—his own bucket spilling over—he looked up at me and said simply, "You suck." To which I had to agree. I do suck. Come springtime, nothing frustrates me more.

I've been privy to the many ways people hunt for morels. I've seen extended families sweeping the woods shoulder-to-shoulder, each filling a bucket in a frantic picker's pace. Someone, usually the father, directs the echelon. Consider it a kind of strip-mining approach executed with the precision of a military operation, one that leaves few standing survivors.

You'll see road hunters prowling the two-tracks on public land. Incredible as it seems, these people can actually spot morels growing in the woods while in a moving car.

I don't know any drive-by pickers. But I know they're out there. On private ground, a drive-by picker will case a likely spot then come back later and drop off a buddy to "do the job."

Most of my friends wander the deep woods alone. They have a few mushroom covers they visit every spring, secret claims they consider their own.

They tell me that morels like to grow in moist earth, in shady stands of young aspen—the same places hunters would expect to find grouse and woodcock. Likewise, the books tell me old orchards and burned-over areas are also good places to look. And, of course, always the warning: "Be careful of the false morel and any morel-like mushroom in the summer and fall."

Nevertheless, I remained jinxed—stunningly luckless. This even though friends grant me open access into their mushroom haunts. The ones who take the most pity on me have actually drawn maps—maps complete with Xs and arrows and kindly advice written in the margins: *Make sure you check that series of grassy hummocks...The edge of the aspens next to the big white pine is always a good place.*

Still I come back empty-handed.

Without my friends, there would be no morels for soups and sauces. None to sauté in butter or to smother a venison tenderloin grilled rare. No mousseline: a concoction of morels, yellow squash, fiddlehead fern, and roasted red pepper.

However, the same friends who are so willing to share their mushroom covers with me do not dole out the actual prize so easily. Once found and dried, morels are never bestowed freely to beggars.

So between us a bartering system has evolved. Thankfully, I'm a better hunter of game than a finder of mushrooms. Among my non-hunting friends who nonetheless enjoy the occasional meal of duck or grouse, a brace or two of either can fetch a bag of morels that, if properly rationed, can last me into the fall.

The only time I've ever done well finding morels is when tagging along with someone. Strange how easily I can spot them when pointed out by a more experienced eye.

"Relax your eyes, like you're staring at one of those 3-D posters," my friend Doug once advised.

Just like that, right off his pointer finger, a half-dozen of the little buggers appeared crowded around the sunny side of a young aspen tree.

Using his technique, last year I found a coal-eyed fawn down by the river, curled up under a cedar tree and woodcock eggs recently hatched, the shells brittle as a spider's web and broken lengthwise, stem to stern.

Other times I've looked so hard at the ground that I've spotted pill bugs scurrying amongst the leaves—salamanders, too, and tiny black ants—but never on a single outing a bounty of morels large enough that I couldn't carry the take in one hand.

So what could possibly be gained from such a daunting task, you wonder? How about the sheer joy of looking for looking's sake? In the woods, aimless concentration is not an oxymoron. Frankly, I don't think people wander the woods and contemplate the black earth underfoot quite enough.

I have looked for morels for enough years that I know I will never be particularly good at it. Still I search the dark woods, slow and silent, every spring studying the ground with the hope of a prospector panning for flecks of gold.

Under the Hex

There are nights in the month of June—specifically during the dusky hatching of the Hex—when I think I would rather enjoy being a trout. I'm talking about a big old hooked-jawed brown, a slab-sided river fish as large as the blade of a canoe paddle. I'm talking about the kind of fish that passes the daylight hours hidden under cut banks and sunken, shadowy logs; the kind of fish that lives a sort of ghost life; the kind of trout hardly ever seen by fishermen and rarely taken on a fly.

That's because big trout like this are predators that prefer meatier morsels—minnows, frogs, salamanders, and, yes, worms—than the dainty little midges and mayflies fly fishermen are so fond of throwing. Big trout almost never feed off the top unless, of course, a critter with some real meat happens by. This is where the largest mayfly in North America comes in—the *Hexagenia limbata*—a gargantuan bug we call the Hex for short.

I read a figure somewhere that on some streams, Hex flies in various forms—nymph, adult, and spinner—constitute as much as 70 percent of the annual trout food intake. Most of the Hex fly's life is passed as creepy-crawly nymph down on the river bottom. Then a transformation happens during a window in summer, cool nights in June and early July, when the nymphs morph and take wing by the millions.

The phenomenon is unique to the Upper Midwest, and specifically northern Michigan. Hex flies are enormous, almost two inches long, excluding a long hairlike forked tail. On our legendary trout streams Up North, the peak of the hatch happens around the middle of June, typically between 9 and 10 o'clock at night, along any stretch of river where the bottom consists of soft silt or marl.

While normal right-thinking fishermen are either home in bed or watching Letterman, real bruiser trout slip from their hidey-holes into the current to gorge themselves on emerging flies and spinners. When the hatch peaks on a good night, the air becomes choked with flies. Beware, you fishermen teetering on the edge of entomophobia; this cloud of insects can get as thick as fog. That means flies in your hair, in your mouth, and crawling in your nose. False casting during this, what anglers call a "blanket hatch," is like swinging a scythe through the numbers. The looping line and the long rod cutting forward and back may strike the bodies of a couple dozen Hex flies at a pass. The noise is a rapid staccato of ticks—*tick-tick-tick-tick-tick*—with the ones you've cut down falling dead on the water where they're quickly gobbled up by rising, ravenous trout.

Should you shine your light skyward, the Hex flies buzzing about look like a million little winged fairies. That's what I see anyway. But that's because, in addition to fits of wanting to be a trout, I'm also a wannabe poet and a geek. The trout, however, is a pragmatist to whom the Hex flies are mere insectile sustenance to the *nth* degree, the fishy equivalent of an all-you-can-eat buffet on oven-roaster chickens. Trout feed on them so voraciously that catching trout can seem easy at times…provided you get the hang of fly-fishing in the dark.

Though everybody on the river carries light at night, either a bright headlamp or a flashlight, you learn to use it sparingly, since to do otherwise is to make your presence known to the fish. Night fishing is best done by your wits and senses. Be prepared for the unexpected, since anything can happen on a river after the sun goes down.

I have a friend who quit night fishing altogether after the singularly traumatic experience of snagging a low-flying bat. Ask him about it today, and the response, "It wasn't good. Not good at all."

Another friend once hooked a beaver that suddenly surfaced under his drifting fly, essentially hooking itself. My buddy went reeling backward, stumbled and fell over a rock midstream as all sixty pounds of that buck-toothed varmint felt the cranial pinch of a #6 Mustad and soaked my buddy proper with one splash of its skillet-shaped tail.

Expect the unexpected when fishing during the Hex hatch. Night fishing can be surreal, but it can also be utter frustration and toil, especially if you're new to casting in the dark. Not to mention expensive, since you're apt to lose more flies (almost $4 a pop) and leader material (I like a simple 3' to 4' section of 10# to 12# tied directly to the fly line) to all the hungry branches and bushes lurking out there in the night.

Did I mention the mosquitoes, how they're a constant torment all night, hawking about for that one bit of your flesh that isn't protected by chemicals?

The fishing is good during the hatch, perhaps some of the best you'll ever find. But it's not easy. After midnight, in the blackness everyday acts seem heroic. I'm thinking about the time my flashlight went dead sometime after midnight, right when the fishing was just taking off. I lost a fly to a fish and actually managed to tie on another, threading the monofilament through the hook eye and everything, all by feel. Then a half-dozen fish later, I had to feel my way two miles back to the car, the whole while convinced something, or someone, was following me.

Everything grows in proportion in the dark. For instance, you hear a lot about 20-inch fish landed during the Hex. Browns of this size are not uncommon, but they're not hiding around every bend either. Most of the river fish anglers claim as 20-inchers probably couldn't eek that on the tape measure unless you heel-stomped them. Figure most to be around that 16- to 17-inch mark, a mighty respectable fish in any water, though especially when landed in the close confines of an average northern Michigan trout stream.

When you're out fishing at night, you occasionally encounter monsters. I'm remembering a time, and a fish, from last year. I had already been fishing out in the dark for a couple of hours, stalking along the bank listening for the rising sounds distinct to giant fish. I had been roving around in the dark for so long, following trails close behind the footsteps of deer up ahead, that I felt as if I had entered some kind of middle zone, a place where my thoughts became as skewed as they are in the morning after waking from a dream.

Sometime after midnight, along some black bend in the upper Boardman, I heard a big fish. In the long silences between its regular rises, I spent a better part of an hour standing in the dark, listening and looking upward, lamenting all the names of constellations I didn't know. There were other fish around—dozens of them, though smaller than a foot or two—slashing at the Hex flies helplessly adrift on the water.

Little fish splash and leap about like…well, little fish do…taking flies willy-nilly over here, over there. But when a big fish rises, it's purposefully executed. The noise is a pounding, full-fisted *glunk!* The rises of a big trout seem at first random, but not after you listen for a while and discern the rhythm. Cast too late or too soon, and a big fish will refuse your fly no matter how flawless the cast.

Any good cast at night is one made totally by feel; same for the drift and the mend of the line. Since you can't see a thing, you must envision the entire process with the confidence in knowing that (by the memory of your muscles learned through repetition of action) everything is playing out in the murkiness as you feel it through the rod. After hours of fishing this way, the eventual strike of a fish seems as if it's come as the culmination of that walking dream.

That was the feeling. With the black sky of a new moon, I may as well have been blind. When the trout rose as I had envisioned it, I raised the rod and became suddenly connected to something alive out there on the other side. The fish led me up river into the darkness, around a bend or two. I gained line, lost line, and regained it again, and once the fish jumped, which I know only because I felt the line go slack followed by the noise of a splash.

Only when I finally had it in-hand did I dare turn on the offensive white light of the headlamp. My eyes took a moment to adjust. The fish lay still on its back, disoriented, while I slipped the hook from the corner of its wicked mouth, feeling the savaged furrows on his back with my fingers.

Given its size, I can only imagine that an eagle had tried to kill this trout. But why was its back only scored and not broken? That's when my imagination started running away.

The trout did not have the sleek lines or slim figure of a river fish but instead the hefty round belly and shoulders—the football shape—of trout born in a lake. But the nearest lake was miles downstream, an easy swim for a fish, perhaps. I'd like to think this trout had been carried here by eagle that lost its grip on this very stretch of river and the fish fell as if deposited here from the heavens.

The trout was as long as my forearm, probably the largest trout I'd ever caught. The scars were fresh, but the fish was fine. I imagined he would carry those marks for the rest of his life. Many anglers I know would have thought such a fish as having the perfect character for a mount. If my outlandish theory about the eagle were true, probably the fish's size and girth had saved him. It made him too heavy for the eagle to hold. It was partly that size that saved him from my claws, but more the fact that I suddenly identified with this beaten up and gnarly old glutton. So I let him go.

Junking

The neighbor is a yard sale junkie. She's utterly hardcore. Anyone can see it by the way she scours the paper for her weekly fix, looking for sales in good neighborhoods, and circling likely hits. I'm an early riser, but even she beats me out of the driveway on the weekends. She is long gone before I've even had my juice. Gone junking. That's what she calls it.

To borrow a term, I'm a bit of a "junker" myself. But a different kind. Some junkers are fond of yard sales, others auctions. I'm a flea market guy, and I'll tell you why.

Contrary to the treasures my neighbor often finds—antique chairs, cast-iron pans, and genuine cork-top blue glass bottles of which she has a sizable collection amassed on her windowsills—I've never had any luck finding anything I like at yard sales. Frankly, they depress me. After all, people hold yard sales when they're moving (not always because they want to), they need money, or they're trying to clean out the garage and make a profit on junk they'd otherwise dump at the landfill.

Maybe I've never had good fortune at yard sales because hardcore junkers like my neighbor have already picked over the goodies and ferreted away the best stuff. By the time I arrive, the only things left are boxes of old paperback romance novels (50¢

each), threadbare clothing, and that ubiquitous green couch with the dubious stain.

As for auctions, they're too impersonal for me, too businesslike what with all the stern faces, the pointing and waving, and the clacking of the gavel that concludes every sale. You can't haggle at an auction. You can't make an offer, walk away, and let the seller stew for a while. Furthermore, I can never keep up with what the auctioneer is saying.

Auctions are also depressing. Unlike at a yard sale where the seller is dying to unload stuff, those behind most auctioned items are often themselves dead. I'm thinking of estate sales where some real bargains can be found. *Great items! Must sell!* Unfortunately, if you could divine an answer you'd probably discover the past owner really didn't plan on parting with his stuff just yet.

Flea markets are different. The best ones are outdoor affairs. Those held inside mean you can go junking anytime. But I think something's lost indoors. For one, the same people are there every week. The same stuff. The feeling is one of shopping at a low-rent strip mall.

Outdoors, you have the bustle and the open air. New vendors set up shop right alongside the regulars. That fresh turnover every week means you never know what you may find, what little treasures you might discover that somebody else is virtually giving away. Of course, therein lies the lore of junking: buying for dirt-cheap items that conjure in us strange feeling of connectedness to the past. Even though we may not always agree on where to find the best junk, all junkers can probably agree on that.

Like me, most people go junking with some specific object in mind. I'm always on the lookout for old wooden fishing lures and handmade duck decoys, cast-iron pans, and until recently a genuine percolating coffee pot, the kind for brewing coffee on the stove the old-fashioned way. Sometimes it's more fun to stay open to the possibilities.

You can learn a lot about people from the stuff they try to hock. The flea market is proof positive that in this world there's a buyer and a seller for just about everything. Consider it the seedy underbelly of the junker's life, but I admit to going to the flea market some Sundays for no other reason than to witness a wonderfully diverse cross-section of humanity. There's an entertainment factor in snooping over somebody else's stuff, engaging in a little artful haggling, then taking time out to watch the other junkers over a Coke and box of greasy French fries or a funnel cake.

Some people don't understand junking at all. When they want something, they buy it new; when they want to get rid of anything, they throw it away. I say more power to them. If nothing else it cuts down the competition come the weekend, which means more junk to go around.

Mosquitoes

I don't know anybody who likes mosquitoes. But like sunburn or poison ivy, who can imagine a summer gone by without them?

The first thing you notice about the mosquitoes in northern Michigan is the sheer number of them. The second thing is that smearing bug-goop all over yourself in an effort to thwart the masses only ends up antagonizing them, so much so that I'm not quite sure if it's the best alternative to simply letting them land on you…at least then you have a chance at murdering the buggers.

Come summertime, my wife Nancy and I get inane pleasure out of killing mosquitoes. We curse them, crush them, squish, squash, and tramp them. Last year we bought one of those pretty blue zapper lights, and I can't tell you how much joy it gives us some nights hearing those little devils pop and burn.

As much as they drive me crazy, I can't help but admire them; the Michigan mosquito (I'm convinced they're a unique strain) has unequaled tenacity. Not bothered in the least by bug sprays, cigar and cigarette smoke, or the noxious flames of our tiki torches and citronella candles, night after night it's never very long before a couple of them breech our defenses.

Nothing is safe from them.

I saw a young buck the other evening, on the edge of a clearcut very near our cabin. His fur was all red, and his neck was thin and delicate. His big, fuzzy antlers had three knobs to a side. All around his body swarmed a gray cloud, an insectile aura, of what else, mosquitoes. The deer came bolting out of the trees, turned a 180 in the middle of the clearing, and lowered his head at the swarm following him. Then he bucked up like a bronco and ran back into the woods, only to reappear a moment later repeating a similar routine.

The only thing I know that actually seem to like mosquitoes are the trout I fish for in summertime. In my fly box, I keep a couple imitations right alongside an assortment of elk hair caddis, pheasant-tailed nymphs, and Adams flies.

A mosquito is one of the most delicate hand-tied flies you've ever seen. The body is wrapped moose mane; the wings, grizzly hen hackle. In fact, if it weren't for the hook the tiny body is wrapped around, the fly would be almost invisible in the palm. Yet a trout will look up and see one of these impostors riding on the current, rise and take it, sometimes over everything else.

Last evening I cast to such a fish.

I was just standing in midstream watching, as fly fishermen so often do, waiting at a favorite bend for something to happen, when the mosquitoes amassed in a cloud around my noggin found the one spot of flesh at the back of my neck not protected by chemicals.

I smacked, cussed, and caught one of the little wretches between my fingers. Her belly bulged with my blood. Such a mosquito, I thought, is to a trout probably one of the most protein-packed nasties in the insect world. As if to confirm the notion, when I flicked her into the current, a trout slashed at the surface where she rode.

For a time this trout would take neither mayfly nor midge, only the gory chum of mosquitoes I tossed to it as fast as I could mash them. Finally, I fixed to the line a four-flusher from my fly box and when the trout rose for it, I lifted the rod gently, setting the hook.

A little brook trout: one for *my* dinner. I brought it midstream where I stood, water swirling round my legs, the current churning with a pulse and gurgling sound like blood, the blood coursing through a vein of a different kind.

34

Behind These Walls

Every year since the move, my wife and I have taken on some major remodeling efforts in our newly acquired home. From minor changes in wall coverings to this year's much-anticipated kitchen renovation, summers are marked by the comings and goings of carpenters, plumbers, and carpet/tile technicians as we endeavor to make another portion of the house more livable (at least by our standards).

Prior to our living here, and as abundantly clear given the obvious remodeling efforts of others, our home showed a good turnaround of owners who my wife and I disparagingly refer to as "the friggin' idiots who lived here before." I understand how snotty this sounds. But I don't care. Unless you live in a brand-new house, you know exactly what I'm talking about.

Concealed behind our walls lies evidence of decades of bad taste and poor judgment. I wouldn't mind so much the former (which can simply be covered up), if it didn't so often marry with the latter and spawn for me so much extra work.

Just once, I would like to find something done right. No slipshod carpentry or jerry-rigged wiring. No walls covered in alternating layers of paint over wallpaper (a piercing pain in the ass to remove). In short, I'm of a mind that no home improvements should ever be tried if you are a lazy or stupid person.

There should be a law.

Just once I would like to embark on some remodeling that didn't require the consultation of various professionals and the accompanying outlay of cash to right some shoddy bit of work done by an overzealous do-it-yourselfer ignorant of their limitations.

I'm tired of the rhetorical questions of carpenters and electricians called in to right the wrongs. I'm tired of getting an eyeful of the plumber's rear end because his pants don't quite fit over his ample belly (when he said, "Let me take a crack at your plumbing problem," I didn't think he meant literally).

But back to the questions...

There are subtle variations, of course. But before any work can commence, the problem must be long considered with the same expression one might wear when regarding a newspaper word jumble or baby's soiled diaper: lips must prune up, heads must be scratched, eyes squinted or averted, before one of three queries must then be muttered:

(1) Well, what do we have here?

(2) Hmm, would you look at that?

(3) Why do you suppose somebody would do that?

I'm thinking of our most recent electrical debacle, the seemingly simple installation of a dimmer switch downstairs that predictably escalated in scope because of past handiwork by a do-it-yourselfer. This was clearly apparent upon discovery of the mess that culminated the trial: a tangle of white, black, red, and green wires that appeared as if it might require a munitions expert to defuse and ultimately proved to confound our man for over $100 worth of his time.

Our latest remodeling project, a radical revamp of the kitchen, also started out simple enough. Therein, always, lies the rub. Several pesky problems turned what was to be a month-long affair into a summer-long endurance test. These involved not one, but three layers of linoleum to tear up in the kitchen; painted-over wallpaper on three of four walls sorely out-of-plumb (indeed, a room devoid of one square corner); and walls with studs placed every 24 inches rather than the standard 16.

Last fall, one of the long-ago previous owners actually stopped by while I was out raking leaves. In the neighborhood "to check out the old place," I suspected immediately by the Magnum P.I. styling (exposed hairy chest, bushy, un-kept mustache, and Hawaiian shirt) that before me was the hipster responsible for the swanky shag carpet and yellow walls in the living room. No doubt, our home was his personal shag pad during the height of the Reagan years.

What I would later recall and curse him for were the other things he admitted doing to the house during his tenure.

"You probably wouldn't believe me if I told you I built that entire addition myself," he said at one point, his remaining shirt buttons confidently popping.

Now, after waking from the nightmare that was our kitchen, I would say unto him, "Just try me."

A month into the kitchen project, I wanted to hunt him down and everyone else who had ever owned the house to tell them what blundering idiots various professionals parading through my house at $50 an hour had confirmed they were. Magnum's addition was the main thing. Grossly out-of-square and without one wall that was plumb, the floor sloped at a grade somewhere between the take-off ramp Robbie Knevil used to leap the Grand Canyon and the highest setting one can achieve on a health club treadmill.

To make the floor matters worse, the pattern chose for the linoleum was some sort of psychedelic mishmash that only exaggerated the fact that the room was out-of-kilter. Guests visiting our home for the first time would step into this room and suddenly grope the walls for something to hold onto. Looking at the floor too long caused mild sensory overload evident by headaches, momentary loss of motor skills, and blurry vision until you managed to stagger out of the room and give your dilated pupils a chance to readjust.

This all said, I fear that down the line when we finally sell this house, the next owners will discover some stupidity behind the walls that I haven't yet uncovered and smite me as I have the lot of those who once lived here. It's the kind of thing that makes me want to pen notes of apology with the salutation To Whom It May Concern, and hide them in all the places we haven't fixed up…and come to think of it, those we have.

The notes will be simple and to the point, saying only:

"It was like this when we found it…honest."

The Great Salmon Lie

I don't know another fish in the rivers of northern Michigan harder to catch than the salmon that begin nosing upstream from the big lake every fall. They are hard to catch because the farther they travel upstream, home to their dying places, the less they bite like ordinary fish if you can coax them to strike at all. But, oh, how people will tell you they do.

I call it "the great salmon lie" since, you see, to catch a salmon up in the headwaters of any river, you need to first find the ones willing (or in a surly enough mood, as is more often the case) to come hell-bent after your spinner, spoon, spawn sac, or fly. This is hard for an angler to do because of the multitude of fish that aren't remotely interested in anything you throw to them.

You might have to cover miles of river, casting over thousands of fish, before you find the one. Seeing the fish right there, so close you can sometimes poke them in the hoary eyes with the end of your pole, is a recipe for frustration unlike any in the angling world.

I hate the word "sporting" as it applies to hunting and fishing. Sports have rules to play by, rules concocted by men. But in hunting and fishing, out there away from the eyes of onlookers, the way by which you come about your quarry is largely your own, called "sporting ethics." But simply "ethics" alone would suffice.

So many salmon blacken the headwaters come fall (in some

cases fish so thick that in jockeying for position they often shoulder one another up onto the banks). It takes nothing less than "the courage of your convictions" not to simply drift your line through the gawping hooked jaws of one, and smartly raise your rod until the hook catches hold of his gnarled, toothy jaw on the other side.

The technique, called "lifting," sounds a tad better than "snagging," but the truth is that they both are the same. The only difference, as every bona fide "snagger" knows, is that with the latter method, anywhere you can fasten onto the fish goes.

Some river guides up here make their living this way, guiding clients to foul-hooked fishes and, in essence, propagating the lie. I fished with enough of them to know that sometimes when guiding for salmon, the real art is not in the fishing but rather in the gyrations necessary to convince the uneducated tourists, who deep down want to believe that these giant fish are easily duped by their gentle touch and flawless presentation. So instead, this bit of treachery is involved.

In any case, I say better to use a pitchfork. Then perhaps when everybody goes home to their Budweiser, the riverbank bushes and trees wouldn't be spaghettied with so much monofilament—a lasting testament to sloppy fishermen and technique—left to tangle robins and ducklings come springtime.

Of course, then most would never experience the real power of salmon, which on a northern Michigan river is the stuff of dreams. Land a salmon up here and you've really accomplished something, since what passes for a river in these parts would more aptly be considered a stream in any other part of the world, or a "crick" where I come from. Tiny, crooked streams like these are perfect for tussling with trout, not 30-pound, demon-eyed salmon that would rather die than come to hand.

The best advice I ever heard on how to land a fish was to simply stay connected to it. One of those things easier said than done. Further, the salmon are so difficult to make bite that they cannot be relied upon to give you much of an education.

If you stay connected, your final dilemma rests in what to do with the fish once it's beached and in your clutches. Anything so difficult to catch and that fights as hard as a salmon—any animal that has it in its blood to fight itself so consistently to the brink of exhaustion and death—I think deserves the best of treatment once it has given its life to you. In the case of the salmon, this doesn't always mean throwing them back.

This sounds of the snagger's logic, that, *Well, they're just gonna die anyway*. But as an upright, eyes-forward, hunter-gatherer type, I believe that sometimes the most respect you can show an animal once it has given itself over to capture is to prepare it for the table and share it with friends the best way one knows how.

I suppose the upshot of all this is respect.

I'm not supposed to condone snagging because of the dishonor it transfers to the fish and riff-raff it brings to the river. Considering the alternative, a side of me can't help admire the utilitarian practicality of it.

Who is more ethical, I wonder? The quiet poacher who goes about his business, leaving no trace, and taking home only what he needs for a meal, or the so-called "sports" who play one fish after another to the point of waxy-eyed death (the fish's, unfortunately not theirs...pity, I know), only to turn them loose, and then later concoct stories about how the fish became connected to the line in the first place.

And so goes the lie.

It's enough to make an honest fisherman take up a pitchfork.

A Good Day

My idea of a good day begins well before sunup, a frosty morning in October. First thing is to stoke the coals in the fireplace and add a couple of pieces of kindling and a big log to take the chill off the house. Feed the dog. Fix the coffee, a big pot that percolates on the stove. Maybe set a couple of strips of bacon and two sunny eggs sizzling in a black iron pan.

After breakfast, I'll set off down a woodsy path to my writing place, a little cabin with a mossy roof, like something a trapper might build, back away from the main house next to a shady stream. Inside there's a big window facing east, overlooking a meadow. My desk, a big one, is cluttered with books, feathers, deer antlers, and pieces of bone. On the sill, on every shelf, little reminders of my wanderings: arrowheads and acorns, interesting pine cones, rocks, pieces of driftwood, and pretty jade and ruby-colored glass picked from the pebbles on the beach.

There's another fire to make here, too, a little one to warm the place. I should like to have a few bird feeders for the nuthatches and chickadees and titmice in my woods. The birds come and go while I sharpen all my pencils, each with a pocketknife, leaving the shavings to fall onto the dusty plank floor. Across the clearing, a deer or two materialize against the treeline, then drift through the grass toward the pines behind the barn.

When the words come, spilling from my head like a prayer, it's like being in a trance, sleepwalking along through the rabble of the mind's voices and separating one of the whispers from the din that moves the hand, mine, as if guided from beyond by a ghost. I'll fill maybe a dozen pages before the armload of wood brought in from outside is gone.

Back in this world, after some good work, lunch is a sandwich wrapped in foil that I slip into my hunting coat. Into the other pocket go a handful of shotgun shells that jostle together with a brassy, satisfying rattle that calls the old dog awake. I tell him we're going looking for a bird and despite two withered hips, he bounces round like a puppy at the news.

Down the footpath again, we break off around the backside of the meadow, ducking through the alder whips, behind the barn where the morning deer are surprised from their beds; white tails flagging, they bound away through the dark pines with those high, graceful leaps. The dog pays them no mind, no more than I pay the grouse that thunders out on the edge of what I will call The Home Cover.

Like the deer, like me, the birds will find refuge in the woods outside my back door. The dog and I hunt the outlying areas, the swampy bottoms and hardwood ridges, the little blueberry patch and the old apple orchard near that old stone wall, what remains of a homestead built by the settler who lived here before.

The dog will rout up a couple woodcock as we wade through the rust-colored ferns and on this day, I will be shooting well enough to tumble at least one of them down. We rest a bit under the shade of some towering maple where we share the sandwich I made. The apple, too, cut into quarters with my pocketknife.

Then off again on the sunny trail leading home, save for one little detour through a patch of pole-sized aspens where I know a cagey gray grouse lives. He will be the kind of grouse that spends a season giving a hunter like me the fits. But today when the bird goes out, I will be ready, only to be surprised to find after the dog carries him back that the bird in my hand is a different one. The big bird, the one I was after, will escape again. The dog puts him up on the edge of the cover, the same old place he always does and too far away for a shot.

My wife, my love, will just be pulling into the drive. We'll make a dinner of the birds and share a bottle of wine on the porch until the sun falls in behind the trees. After all these years, we still hold hands. When she smiles, I feel a flutter in my chest. And it makes me smile, too.

My perfect day is all imagined, you understand. For one thing, I never write or shoot as well in real life as I do in my dreams. But there are moments, like those memories of a smile and a bird gone away over the trees, just as there are daydreams of a place where I might work and live in solitude, yet not alone.

Camp Music

When it comes to music, my appreciation of styles runs wide thanks to the broad exposure I regularly receive in the most unlikely of places: hunting camp.

Now you probably think musical appreciation is a subject lost on most hunters, but I'll have you know I tramp the woods with a rather eclectic group of friends: parrotheads and deadheads, country bumpkins, classic rockers, and a number of folks I regard as totally out there not only musically but on every imaginable fringe. Some are wannabe DJs (a bothersome affliction at get-togethers, akin to watching a puffed-up shopping-mall rent-a-cop living out the fantasy of being a real live policeman). For them, the selection of music listened to while away at camp is of nearly equal importance to what manner of malted and fermented beverages should be indulged in (after the hunt, of course) during our woodland hiatus.

Again, I realize this runs counter to the stereotype most people hold of hunters. Everybody knows hunters only care about getting crocked at camp, typically on the cheapest rotgut they can find. Hunting camp is supposed to be the yokel's domain, a place where the only song you're liable to hear is a nightly chorus of wheezy-breathing boozers snoring and cutting farts while passed out on the couch. Hunting does make for strange bedfellows, especially here in northern Michigan where everybody seems to do it regardless of their education, taste, or station in life.

I have been to a fair number of hunting camps even though I've never had a cabin of my own. Going where I'm invited, I'm what you might call a "floater." Dishing about like that, you learn it's best not to complain about anything, least of all the music played at camp. When it comes to music, if you don't have a place to hang your rifle, either you ditch all stereophonic cynicism and learn not to bitch about what's on the hi-fi or you find yourself hunting a lot from home. Maybe that's why I learned long ago to muster the same enthusiasm singing Johnny Cash as I do when hammering out the perfect air drum solo during the long version of Iron Butterfly's "In-A-Gadda-Da-Vida." In the process, not only have I learned to appreciate all manner of song, after a good day in the mountain—passing the bottle around in time with some tunes in the background—I've also found that almost any kind of music is agreeable if the company is too.

Though our differences are best summed up in the songs we bring to camp, it's not my purpose to argue one sound over another. "Writing about music is like dancing about architecture—it's really a stupid thing to want to do," said Elvis Costello.

Music adds another flavor to camp. And a song sure can take you back. A goodie came on the radio yesterday that reminded me of heading to hunting camp the first time with the boys. I was about thirteen. The invitation came through a school friend.

All I remember of the drive is that we stopped a lot for gas, food, and supplies. The stereo was blaring Jimi Hendrix. I was sitting in the backseat between the speakers, where I felt the volume of Jimi's guitar riffs fracturing my vertebrae. My buddy's uncle was happy and had a lot of money to throw around. We also had to keep stopping so he could use the bathroom, which I thought was great because my mother didn't believe in going to the bathroom—not ever and especially on long trips—not to mention listening to loud rock music and hoggishly eating like we were.

Between my buddy and me, we downed a couple dozen cheeseburgers, a few pounds of fries, and a bag or two of barbequed potato chips. We washed it all down with messy swigs of Coke gulped straight from a two-liter bottle. The Uncle had a bottle of his own. Every time he threw one back, he sighed a refreshing "Aaaaaaa!" and wiped his chin with one manly swipe of the sleeve. I started doing the same. We were living large and rockin' out.

When we finally reached the cabin, the party was a lot more subdued. Men were playing cards under a dim overhead light, talking about deer and hunting and arguing to the point of cussing one another about whether this ridge or that ridge was going to be the better spot to see a buck come first light. I sat enraptured, taking it all in. If you wanted something to eat or drink, you didn't ask, by God, you just moseyed on over to the kitchen and got it. It was fun.

But the Uncle got restless. After a few losing hands, he mentioned wanting to go into town. The card game fell apart, one player at a time, until eventually the trucks all rumbled away, spitting gravel out of the drive and leaving my buddy and me there all alone.

We had old hunting magazines to look at and tapes from the ride up to listen to. I should probably preface the rest of this by saying that my friend and I weren't a couple of delinquents…just two young boys curious about being men. On the table was a bottle of Teachers that the card players had been drinking, and that's probably all the information anyone needs to figure out what happened next.

Suddenly everything seemed so silly. I remember going outside and forgetting why, and when I wandered back in and asked my friend, "You remember why I went out there?" my face hurt because we laughed so long about it. The littlest things made us giddy. We listened to one tape and got hooked on the first song: Blue Swede's now particularly annoying rendition of B.J. Thomas' "Hooked on a Feeling."

At the time, the chanting of the opening chorus struck us as the funniest thing yet and made us even more punchy. We played it over a dozen times until suddenly our merriment ended. It seemed like one minute we were chanting *Ouga chaka! Ouga-Ouga-Ouga chaka!* Then all of a sudden, we both wretched forward and did.

Twenty years later, many songs bring back memories but none quite as vivid as that one. I can still smell and taste that cheap blend. Though I'd like to tell you more about the music that's made better those hard days of hunting, made stronger the bonds of friendship, and made more restful the evenings passed by the fire, I can't. Blue Swede's "Hooked on a Feeling" just got stuck in my head again and I can't tell you how it makes my stomach turn.

Tracks

*I know which way a mind wended this morning, what
horizon it faced, by the setting of these tracks; whether it
moved slowly or rapidly, by the greater or less intervals and
distinctness, for the swiftest step leaves yet a lasting trace.*
—Henry Thoreau, 1841

I'm a lover of stories so, naturally, I'm a lover of tracks.

It's one reason I enjoy winter so much. The woods after a freshly fallen snow, every time, feel to me clean and quiet and made new again, what with so many tracks, so many new trails—make that *tales*—to follow.

I have a red fox living in the woods behind the house. Though I've never seen him, I know he's made it another year. Every winter, after every new dusting of snow, I find his tracks in all the same places. He likes the rock pile behind the barn—no doubt, for the mice he finds there. And the brush piles, too, along the edge of the field—they make good shelter for all sorts of game, and I've been building on a half-dozen of them for three seasons.

Early this morning I followed the fox's path around to each one, until the tracks told of a rabbit surprised. White belly fur hung low in the Juneberry like cotton balls, stuck fast to the snow with icy beads of blood.

In winter, the coyotes move in and run the creek bottom in pairs…strange, since fox and coyotes don't get along any better than the crows get along with the hawk and the owl. This makes me think that my fox is an old, cagey one—that, likely, he's lived on this run-down farm a lot longer than I have.

But back to the coyotes. At this time of year, the swamp holds them as if it holds its secrets. In winter, I sleep with the windows in the bedroom open just a crack and can often hear them yipping and howling to one another outside. Rarely are they seen in the daylight. The snow tells me that they often circle the house at night, just beyond the glow of porch light in the backyard. Snow also reveals what I have always known: that coyotes are opportunists who would just as soon feed on the kibble left in the cat's bowl outside the barn as take down a sickly fawn.

In the snow, I find coyotes taking up the scent of deer and following the deer tracks, each trail like a chain of tiny black hearts. I've never found, not even once, where the coyotes have taken down a healthy whitetail—at least not in winter. In my swamp, the deep snow and cold kill more deer than those little gray dogs do.

It's all there in the tracks, which I read as if they were a foreign language. The stories they tell are older than cave paintings, certainly older than the first human thought that inspired our own dialect of throaty clicks and guttural growls.

On winter walks, I carry in my pocket a mud-stained, water-worn, dog-eared copy of Olaus Murie's *Field Guide to Animal Tracks*. When I was a boy, the book was my Rosetta Stone. Even now, I go to it when trying to decipher some of the messages left for me in the snow.

When I was small, I used to circle back on my own tracks, and found that by looking at them—I mean *really* looking at them—I could tell exactly what I was doing at the time my foot made the imprint in the snow. Like some form of primitive time travel, each imprint took me back to the exact thought, the very thing I was gazing at or contemplating upon its making.

I share my little piece of property with the fox, the badger, the owl, and the big round-hoofed buck that beds in the alders down by the river—animals that I know are there yet have never seen, creatures that know the moon's path better than I know the sun's. Perhaps I've always been a bit envious of them and that other place they inhabit—a world their tracks hint at but one I can only imagine, that I'm desperate to learn more of, but can never truly know.

Waiting for the Mail

It feels like I'm always waiting for the mail. I work at home, which means the afternoon mail run is both a pivotal point and cosmic center to my workday. You see, that little box at the end of the drive is where my paychecks appear. It's also where letters of rejection and bills marked past due arrive in despairingly unequal proportion. Money isn't everything, but living can be precarious without it. So after a visit from my postal carrier, the mood of the day tends to go either way: happy, happy, happy or very, very sad.

A run of bad luck found me thinking about the mail much more than usual. Christmas was less than a month away. Some promised money was slow in coming and messages left on my editor's answering machine were going unanswered.

Enter Dan. Dan is my mailman. He visits the house every day around noon, later on Mondays. I've grown so attuned to his regular visits, marked by the metallic pings and distinct rattle of his car, that no matter how busy musing, or lost in story or the battle to save Earth in this fascinating new Internet version of Space Invaders, I snap awake at the noises like a dog whose owner has finally come home.

I think it strange how few people make an effort to know their mail carrier. Deep down, I know mine is just a messenger and that cubby with the red metal flag out front is just a box. But I've always been a little superstitious about luck and believe to some extent that the god of good tidings can sometimes be coerced through a little sacrifice. Chalk it up to the human condition. No doubt this same sense of helplessness is the stuff that used to make Indians dance for buffalo, or island people throw perfectly good virgins into the fires of an angry volcano.

I used to leave gifts for Dan. Always around the holidays, so he wouldn't get the wrong idea. Festive nuts and Santa-shaped cookies pinched from my wife's kitchen, that kind of thing. Such niceties make for good neighbors, but rarely had the desired effect on what mail Dan left for me.

Good news comes when it comes. I knew Dan's face well enough to recognize him down at the general store. If I passed him headed the other way, tucked in behind the passenger-side steering wheel of that blue Cutlass Sierra with the yellow light on top, we would wave…but then again, out here in the country, everybody waves at everybody. He might spot me a stamp here and there when I absentmindedly placed an envelope in the box without one, but I wouldn't exactly call us pals.

Yet Dan could tell I was waiting for something. If not for the days I stood at the end of the drive waiting for him, always with a cool elbow leaning on the mailbox, then certainly after he handed off the latest stack of envelopes and I, after furiously fanning through them, asked with an audible sigh why he was holding out on me.

"Can't find what you're looking for, huh?" he said.

"Maybe it fell down between the seats?"

"Don't think so," he said, pursing his lips, considering. "I'll see what I can do tomorrow."

With that, he drove on.

Well, a couple tomorrows came and went. After a renewed flurry of calls to my New York editor, I came home to a message on the machine. The hoots and hollers in the background suggested some sort of Christmas Eve office revelry.

"Bob-ba-rino old buddy. The check's in the mail."

So this is what I did: I waited some more. The closer it got to Christmas, the more colorful were the envelopes that began appearing in the mailbox. Pretty red and green ones. But instead of well wishes from relatives I hardly know, instead of dollar bills inside that fluttered to the pavement when I opened the cards, most contained snappish little notices with words—**90 Days Past Due**, **Collection Department**, and **Due Now**—done in bold-face so as to leave little ambiguity as to the sender's mood or intentions.

Even though Santa was on a tight budget this year, we had plenty of merriment around our house Christmas Morn. But with the presents opened and the house quiet again, I was back to brooding—sitting alone in the living room, mentally calculating the cost of the mess.

I didn't hear the knock at the door, but later that morning found the envelope taped there containing the check I had been waiting for. A note: *Came in late on yesterday's truck. Special delivery. Merry Christmas. Dan.*

I probably would have hugged old Dan if he were standing there. As it is, I plan to do him one better. But first, I have to get a bigger mailbox, something with ample room to squeeze a nice, healthy virgin inside.

The Perfect Tree

It's Christmas. Not exactly the time of year for getting ticked off by your fellow man. But that's exactly how I felt after reading an article about the work scientists are doing to genetically engineer the "perfect" Christmas tree, a tree with, and I quote, "good needle characteristics, straight trunk, upswept branches, well-formed crown, nice color, and fast growth."

Now I'm all for science and making a buck, but the idea! It was enough to make me stand up and topple my highball of holiday cheer. In some way I couldn't quite put my finger on, this exemplified something wrong with Christmas nowadays. So call it a small act of rebellion, but right there I decreed that this year in our house would not stand one of those already outrageously overpriced, pre-cut Christmas trees. By God, I would cut down a tree of my own, a tree from the forest where I believed already perfect trees are grown.

It was a romantic idea that immediately appealed to the hunter-gatherer in me. The fact is, you can't just go out and start hacking down trees, not on public ground anyway. You need a piece of private property, or in my case, an understanding friend who, though he eyed the ax in my hand suspiciously, nevertheless agreed to give me the key to his gate.

My wife was also skeptical but at the last minute she decided to come along, I think probably to make sure I didn't hurt myself.

"It's going to be an adventure, Sugar Plum," I said, "one of those things we'll never forget."

"That's exactly what I'm afraid of, Charlie Brown," she said.

So we traveled over the river and through the woods, me leading the way with my trusty double-bit angled confidently over one shoulder. We set aside an afternoon for the looking. In and out in an hour, I smugly thought. We would have the thing home $40 richer and decorated in time for cocktail hour.

Before that day, I would have guessed I'd seen in my wanderings about a bazillion Christmassy-type trees growing wild in the northern Michigan woods. Up here, the land is evergreen, spruce and pine galore. Maybe that's what riled me so. Why do we always have to buy our yuletide cheer?

Now, I know we all breathe easier because Christmas trees are commercially grown. The same article that drove me into the woods also noted that farms nationwide provide the daily oxygen requirement for eighteen million people. Here in Michigan, Christmas trees are good for the economy. Some twelve hundred growers provide around 20 percent of the national market. Real trees, a renewable resource, don't require fossil fuels to produce, unlike artificial trees. Also, tree farms promote soil stability and provide habitat for wildlife.

Enough tree trivia. Like everybody else, I was just looking for the perfect (there's that word again) tree that defines me as a person. Only I decided to take the road less traveled, or in this case, a muddy footpath that ended in a swamp.

We slogged around for hours, finding only cedars and ratty-looking jackpines. Then there appeared one little spruce alone in a clearing. I had that stomach flutter that you get when finally stumbling upon something you had given up for lost. Nancy felt it too. That "I-told-you-so" glare she'd been wearing dissolved into a smile. The tree, a squat little guy with unruly branches, would have suited us just fine at the moment. But of all the bad luck, almost the entire backside of the tree was gone, bark stripped and branches broken, by what was undoubtedly one dandy whitetail buck.

Nancy was crestfallen. But I, the consummate tightwad, remained undaunted.

Just like that, it occurred to me, *What if we took home a swamp cedar?* I finally had to ask. At last, the long way of bringing us back around to my living room where this whole little wandering began.

I couldn't find any references to early settlers using swamp cedars as Christmas trees. Truth is, the only mention I did locate was something that said white cedars emit a smell—a stink—when cut down and brought into a warm house. I kept this little tidbit to myself and in the end found it totally untrue, most likely a bit of propaganda cooked up by radicals affiliated with the National Christmas Tree Association to discourage the public from making an annual end-run around convenience. (Note: I made this group up, only to later find such an association actually does exist—that's right...*scary*, isn't it?)

But why not a cedar, I ask you? Granted, the only time ours appeared to have any of the characteristics men of science are supposedly striving for was when I peered at it through the fish-eye lens of an empty glass after the wife and I had toasted our stick-to-itiveness a half-dozen times.

Conservatively adorned with white twinkle lights and ornaments, capped off with that special wooden star that Nancy picked up from the flea market for a dime, our bushy-looking tree was not only delightfully non-traditional; it was free. Back in a festive mood, reclined triumphantly in my chair, I could once again rest easy, knowing all was right with the world.

Life and Taxes

The winter all but past (nothing to write home about) and you would think the worst possible part of living Up in Michigan was over. Not so fast—it is tax season, a particularly disagreeable time when the government requires an accounting for how you spend your daylight hours. When you're broke, those forms have a way of calling career choices into question, not to mention the fact that the pay scale in northern Michigan is so grossly out-of-whack with the rest of the country.

A friend once said that you don't move to northern Michigan to "get ahead in your field." You come here to stand in a field. Ours is a tourist town come summer, a picture-postcard community that overlooks a Caribbean blue finger of Lake Michigan, Grand Traverse Bay. Which brings to mind another old saying, "A view of the bay is half the pay."

If only that miserable old saw were true.

There's better opportunity, bigger money, elsewhere.

Come tax season, that hodgepodge of numbers reckoning income and loss is not only depressing, it also confirms what my wife has been saying all year. Instead of trying to quantify it with pay stubs and receipts, I'd rather we remind ourselves why a life up here is worth living by taking an inventory of another kind.

It's probably a good exercise no matter where you live. Topping my own list are all the obvious things that make the North so appealing to weekend tourists: the intoxicating wide-openness of the country; the sunny beaches and good, clean air; and, of course, the unhurried pace of life in a small town.

I'm proud of the friendships made. Friends naturally become surrogates for family when you're lacking those kinds of ties to the place you live. But then I also like the people of northern Michigan in general. What's not to like about folks in the habit of saying "Excuse me" and "Thank you" and "How do you do"? I like people who look me in the eye when they talk and wave over the steering wheel when crossing paths on a winding country road.

I remember that first winter here, how I marveled at how the snow fell, and kept falling, like nothing I had ever seen back East. The gas gauge in the truck was on the fritz and, coming home from work one night, I unknowingly ran the tank dry. It wasn't quite in the middle of nowhere, but close. The wind blew something awful—not merely sheeting the snow sideways but actually blowing it back *up*!

Now if you've always lived here, it probably doesn't seem out-of-the-ordinary that somebody stopped to give me a lift. Nor does it probably strike as odd that this person—a young lady with two small children, no less—not only waited for me while I sheepishly filled a container with a gallon or two but also drove me back to my heap of a car, thus seeing to it that I hardly got my loafers wet.

Who were those folks, the half-dozen or so, who every time appeared with jumper cables, shovels, and tow ropes to bail out of the ditch or a jam the same old dope with Pennsylvania plates? I wonder. I never again want to live in a place where kindness to strangers is the exception rather than the norm.

Give me trout streams, big woods, and towns with Indian names. I need a country wild with wolves and moose and rumors of mountain lions, the kind of place where a young hunter taking his first whitetail buck makes the front page of the local news.

Here, the country, not the calendar, tells me when the seasons change. Spring is warm rain and a skein of geese heading home. Summer: a sunny day on the beach. Autumn is a harvest moon and leaves the color of fire and sun. Winters are gray, snowy, and cold.

When work saps everything from you, place has a way of filling you up again. If you're like me, you need to head outside when in want of a little perspective.

So, today found me standing alone, waist-deep in a river, casting to trout, where the ebb and flow of the current pulled all dismal notions of impending poverty away. Then it began to snow, one of those freak April storms, with wafting flakes as big as silver dollars. I held my palm out to catch one. But just like that other sort of wealth, I was surprised to find how quickly this one, too, melted away in my hand.

The Greatest Little Store in the North

I want to tell you about my favorite little store, the quintessential northern-Michigan small-town store. It happens to be right down the road from where I live. It's called The Lake Ann Grocery. Our town (actually, Lake Ann is a "village" according to the sign) is a tiny one; imagine a main street with a Mayberry feel. We have one quaint little bank, one diner-style eatery, and one yellow blinking light to mark the center of town. A handful of homes are scattered amongst tall green maples and white pines, and just through their breezy tops, you can even see the big blue water of the lake that lends the place its name.

The store is right there, too—you can't miss it. It sits invitingly across the street from a small, anonymous post office and next door to the town hall and an old brick firehouse (usually with a placard sign out front announcing that Saturday's pancake breakfast along with a band of firefighters standing around, thumbing their red suspenders and generally doing firemen stuff). This saloon-style building looks straight out of an old Hollywood western.

I've never been much on towns, yet for some reason I've grown to like this place so much, it's not hard to find a reason to head down there every day. A new habit of mine is to take an hour's lunch—maybe some crackers, salami and cheese, and a can of Coke to wash it down—out on the picnic bench in the sunshine. There I can watch the waves on the lake, say hello to neighbors I recognize as they come and go, or just sit studying whatever is advertised on the marquee out front. There's always some new item or exciting bargain: Delmonico steaks, pork tenderloins, homegrown cucumbers, rhubarb, blueberries, and sweet cherries in summertime.

But Lake Ann Grocery is more than just some rinky-dink spot to buy those perishable odds and ends when you're loath to drive the twenty-odd miles to the nearest supermarket. Ours is the real deal general store. From fennel seeds to fish hooks, brake fluid to Bordeaux. I can't remember coming out of the place without having found every oddball item on my list. That includes all manner of hardware: a full stock of nails, screws, hinges, and hasps, along with things I have yet to be able to conjure a need for—compression and flare fittings, grommets, toilet seat hinge bolts, gasket shellac compound, and six sizes of nipple pipes.

Nipple pipes!

Now I know the real value of a small-town store is measured by its convenience and for the variety of items found on the shelves. But what I really like is how the wooden screen door creaks when you open it and satisfyingly slams when it shuts. There's also that merry jingle of sleigh bells to announce your presence to the proprietors of the place.

John and Sandy are definitely the neighbors to call when short on something and pressed for time. John, a jolly, white-bearded man somewhere in his fifties and Sandy, a tall, pretty lady whose smile reminds me of my second-grade teacher Mrs. Archibald, are usually somewhere inside restocking shelves.

I like those delightfully crowded aisles, the creak of the wooden floorboards under my feet as I weave between stacks of comforting clutter. For me, prowling up and down them is yet another one of the many facets of life Up North that I enjoy.

Every country store should have at least one cat and this one usually has two running around. And this: In the middle of the place sits an old Alaska National woodstove that really works and round during the colder months finds shirt-and-tie businessmen warming their hands alongside country bumpkins in bib-overalls and blaze-orange hats.

The place is small but there's room for everything and everybody. I think that's what I like best. We have a community here, and this little store is at the heart of it. I consider it a bonus that Lake Ann Grocery is the kind of place where nobody stares should a late-night craving for ice cream send me down to the store clad in my PJs.

So if you're ever up this way, stop on in and look around. Don't be afraid if you see some harried guy standing in line wearing sleepy-time pants, fuzzy slippers, and clutching a pint of Chubby Hubby in one hand and a nipple pipe in the other. It's only me.

Working the Sticks

People sometimes ask why, given all the time I fritter away on the water—hunting, fishing, and recreating—I don't use a motor to get around. My little nephew, up for a bit of bluegill fishing last weekend, looked downright dejected watching me wrestle the canoe off the truck after we arrived at the lake. "Uncle Bob, don't you have a real boat?" he asked. I was, in a word, dumbfounded. Amazing, I thought, how the lack of a little gas-powered propulsion so often casts the seriousness of my endeavors into question.

But I do love to row. My favorite boat right now is a 16-foot Old Town canoe. It's wide-beamed, deep-bottomed, a real hulk of a boat. It came with a seat in the middle and set of oarlocks, so it can be paddled or rowed. It's heavy. The thing powers through skim ice on the duck marsh loaded down with decoys and a couple of unruly retrievers. And stable. I've taken it out on Lake Michigan in good-sized rollers to troll the old-fashioned way for salmon and steelhead, while on smaller lakes I can even stand up in the thing when fly casting back in the tangles where the big bass like to hide.

I heard a figure once, that Michigan has over 11,000 inland lakes and ponds. There are dozens more unnamed, I'm sure of it, especially when you consider all those beaver ponds and backwater sloughs hidden away deep in the dark woods of the North—places where motorboats can't or aren't allowed to go. What of the rivers, and for that matter, the miles upon miles of Great Lakes shoreline?

The writer Bill Mason might as well been talking about the face of Michigan when he described his native Canada by saying, in part, that to "study the geography carefully, you come away with the feeling that God could have designed the canoe first and then set about to conceive a land in which it could flourish."

In my canoe, I can head off in whatever direction my imagination leads. Burdened by a motor, I suspect I would look at these wanderings differently; after all, make a pricey investment like that and naturally, you want to milk every penny from it. That means sticking only to those places where the water is deep and open enough to bear down on the throttle.

One of the big reasons I hunt and fish is to get away from noise, commotion, and those manmade things that never seem to work right. I want to be out on the water exploring any distant corner of the pond that interests me, trying to make sense of what the ducks are doing or what the fish are eating, not stuck at home in the garage, unable to make heads or tales of a greasy mess of clogged valves and confusing colored wires.

And how about the romance of rowing? I'm thinking of all those Hemingway stories I used to love. Whether trolling for lake trout, contemplating the end of something with a girlfriend named Marjorie, or heading across the bay with his father and Uncle George to the Indian camp, I somehow doubt Nick Adams could have pondered the imponderable as compellingly over the whine of a two-stroke and the noxious smell of gas fumes and oil exhaust.

Thirty-one is hardly over-the-hill, but you're definitely not a kid anymore. To listen to my wife is to believe my blatant anti-motor bias is some indication of a midlife crisis looming on down the road. If so, I say better to engage oneself in youthful activities rather than trying to throttle through midlife on the back of a Harley Davidson or top down in some candy-apple-red convertible wearing cool-guy shades and a pair of those silly little sheepskin driving gloves.

I cling to the naïve notion that a day on the water is sweeter when you pay for your pleasure with a little bit of muscle and sweat. So as long as my back and arms are up to the task, I intend to keep working the sticks.

Rowing is good for the body, good for the mind. When asked why he went on a four-week, five-hundred-mile expedition down the Churchill River in Northern Saskatchewan, the voyager Omond Solandt replied, "I went along to iron out the wrinkles in my soul."

But try to explain all this to a twelve-year-old. My nephew just shrugged; Uncle Bob had drifted off on another one of his tangents again. Rowing can also do that to you; it puts you in a mood for some serious reflection. It was unlucky for him, being stuck out there with me in the middle of the lake, rowing to the next hole nice and slow. We had plenty of quiet, plenty of time. I was on a roll and I had him good and proper.

City Fishing

A non-fisherman just passing through would find nothing too spectacular about the river flowing through downtown Traverse City. That's where the Boardman fizzles out, its tired waters corralled between concrete walls and brick buildings until finally emptying into the west arm of Grand Traverse Bay.

Nevertheless, I can't think of another city in the country where you can drop your truck at a downtown garage to have a sticky starter replaced, grab your fishing rod out of the back on a lark, and not only be on a river in as much time as it takes to walk a couple of blocks, but actually catch some fish. Big and, often, exotic fish. Depending upon the time of year, you can peer down from atop the Union Street Bridge into the water below and spot king salmon or steelhead, walleye or perch, pike, gar, brown, and lake trout all fresh out of Lake Michigan.

You also see lots of suckers and carp and, like any urban fishing hole, the usual underwater assortment of tires, rusted iron, Frito bags, and Budweiser cans. The Union Street dam forms what looks like a big concrete swimming pool where black water churns up sudsy trails of unhealthy looking white foam. Not exactly the backdrop of a classic fishing tale, but then anybody can find an ear when discussing the glamorous fishes that inhabit the pristine and more storied waters of the northern Michigan countryside.

Instead, I'm here to sing about city fishing.

Growing up a thousand miles east of here, I learned about fishing like a million other suburban boys: by wetting a line almost every day after school in water hemmed in by apartment buildings and parking lots. The North promised something else—namely, trout—though I'll admit I knew little of trout at the time. I was bona fide trash fisherman with mostly book-learned knowledge of the fish (and fish-inspired tales and legends) that inhabited the wild rivers up here.

For instance, I knew that the Adams fly, the most versatile dry fly pattern ever conceived, was invented on the Boardman River some twenty-odd miles from my new home outside Traverse City. The Au Sable, due east, is where Trout Unlimited was born. Hemingway fished here. And that's just for starters. The upshot is, with nobody around to educate me, I had to start over and found fishing in town a comfortable place to begin.

I've never been a big fan of city living. But when you're deep in the concentration of fishing, the rattle of traffic, the rotting smell of back-alley dumpsters and diesel exhaust, and the occasional heckler critiquing your technique (I'm remembering an errant cast that landed my fly in a tree and some teenie-bopper on the bridge yelling, "Hey, pretty sure the fish are down a little lower. Har! Har!") has a tendency to dissolve away. Although never totally alone, overall I concur with the writer Greg Keeler who said, "If wilderness is where people aren't, then there's plenty of it in the middle of the darkest dankest of cities and towns."

I caught my first lake trout at the Union Street dam over lunch hour one snowy December afternoon. Actually, I caught three, one right after the other on a Day-Glo green egg pattern without another soul around to witness the coup. Months later and downriver under the bridge, where the boardwalk ends and there was a sandy hole under the weeping branches of a willow tree, I caught my first steelhead, fresh from the bay and silver-sided, though barely legal. Again, nobody was around to see, save for a bum digging around the library trash bin looking for cans and chewing on a half-eaten sandwich of suspect origin. High on a heady mixture of generosity and pride, I offered up the fish.

"Bah," he said, "I wouldn't eat anything come out of there."

City fishing is like that, surrounded by stigma regardless of your station in life. Even my fishing friends look down on any piscatorial activity within the city limits, regarding it as mere child's play. Having never been the kind to take myself too seriously, maybe that's why I like it so. For one thing, at my Union Street hole there is always the possibility of the unexpected surprise. I caught a submarine-sized carp there one time while stripping streamers for trout. Another time, a pike as long as an ax handle on, of all things, a dough ball. With so many different fishes swimming in the water, I never know what I'm going to catch, which, come to think of it, is exactly the kind of wonder that got me into fishing in the first place.

So I started fishing in a city and to the city I sometimes return. It might only be for an hour between errands or in a spare moment before some appointed hour. If you're like me, sometimes you just have to get out and fish if only to feel reconnected for a time to more than just whatever happens to be pulling at the end of your line.

Jimson Hollow

Down in Jimson Hollow, you'll find rabbits in every tangle of briars and under every pile of brush. The best time to go there is in October after a good night of rain; the ground is wet then and good for stalking. I like to take my bow and a couple arrows, but I guess a single-shot .22 would be all right. But it would have to be old and beaten up a little, and I shouldn't have to tell you that scopes aren't allowed.

It's best to find a deer trail (they're not hard to find), and follow it down into the hollow. You'll probably have to get down on your hands and knees in some places, and in others, you'll be down on your belly.

When you come upon any place that looks big enough to hide a rabbit, stop and look real close. Look for that little tuft of white that is the rabbit's tail, or that soft gray line that is the curve of the rabbit's back. Maybe you'll see his eye, that's what I always see first. The rest of him will appear like some kind of magic.

You have to be patient to hunt rabbits in Jimson Hollow. If you don't have patience, you'll probably walk past every one. If you think you can go in there with a dog and a shotgun and come out with the limit of rabbits, well, you wouldn't be the first to try. Dogs get lost in Jimson Hollow; sometimes the brush just swallows them up.

Men with shotguns are always looking for a running rabbit, so they don't see the ones that hold still. They don't see the rabbits that crawl so far into the tangles that the light can't even get to them. Halfway through Jimson Hollow, the man with the shotgun will stop and whistle for his dog. If the dog is a beagle, he'll hear it and it will be on a rabbit, but it won't be in Jimson Hollow. The man will smile, fingering the safety on his pump-gun, waiting for his dog to bring the rabbit back around. But after a little while, when the baying of the beagle sounds as far away and as soft as the wind, he will realize that the dog isn't ever coming back around. He might even curse his dog for running deer. But it's not deer that the dog is chasing; it's a Jimson Hollow rabbit.

I forgot to tell you. Jimson Hollow's younger population of rabbits do run but only in straight lines, way out ahead of any hunter and always away from Jimson Hollow.

If you don't have patience, all is not lost. Along with a rabbit or two, patience is the only thing you can take from there. You learn patience by watching the owls. Learn to see like the owls and you'll find the sitting rabbits, not just in Jimson Hollow, but anywhere. Once you learn what the owls have to teach, you'll probably leave the gun under the bed and hunt the rabbits in Jimson Hollow with a bow. You'll know you're doing all right when the rabbits you find don't even know you're there.

The eye is the best thing to aim for on a sitting rabbit. Once you find it, look for something inside, like that tiny speck of light. When you find that, concentrate on it until there is nothing else in the world; if you think about pulling the string to your face, or how the bow feels in your hand, you've probably missed the rabbit even before the release. But if you don't think about any of it, your arrow might very well fly as swift and quiet as the owl and slip through the hole in the brush and find the sparkle of the rabbit's eye.

After you've placed the arrow back into your quiver, find your knife and take the rabbit to the nearest stump or fallen log. Pull some of the white belly-fur from the rabbit and place it close beside. Now make a long slit where the fur used to be and take out what's inside. Set this atop the fur. It is something for the owls.

Now put the rabbit into your jacket, or tie it to your belt with a strip of leather. If you're like me, you probably won't see any more rabbits after the first. Usually, I'm walking too fast after that. I like the way the rabbit feels hanging there on my belt. The way it bumps against my leg with every footstep is something like a heartbeat. It's subtle and pleasant and it carries me the rest of the way through Jimson Hollow.

Gray Days

When I recollect my best days hunting, the memories dawn mostly cloudy and gray. I'm talking about the gray days and cloudy skies preceding a storm. Every hunter knows that animals sense and instinctually move before the coming of a storm. I think the same urge stirs in me.

Give me unbroken skies white as a bed sheet; it makes me feel so alive. I like my woods a little misty and my fields wrapped in a frosty October fog. Give me a downpour looming in the forecast. Maybe even a little rain the night before. That's the best: lying in bed listening the night before a hunt, listening to the raindrops ticking on the window, falling heavy at first then ebbing away to a drizzle just before dawn.

I like those chilly autumn days between storms. "Partly cloudy skies with a chance of rain." I almost quiver when the weathermen say that or warn of a front blowing in from the west.

Instead of holing up somewhere warm and dry, I want to be outside. I want to be out stalking. A favorite swamp I hunt is best seen in the hours before it rains, especially up under the white pines, the golden ground, where the fallen needles make my footsteps seem lighter, quieter, than a fox. It's like hunting in that middle zone, a dawn that seems to linger on forever, not quite night and not exactly day.

In the swamp, farther down the hill near the beaver pond, where the aspen trees, crooked and white as skeleton bones, bend along the cloudy bank, I once came upon a tiny woodcock taking a sip of rainwater pooled in a curled maple leaf. A wind blew that fall day, a good strong wind all at once from everywhere. The muted colors: aspen leaves colored like the sun mixed with the orange from the sugar maples and the ones fluttering down from the rusty tops of the oaks. Leaves swirled and filled the air like ticker-tape during a parade. That woodcock, when it finished drinking, fluttered upward, itself looking like a tumbling leaf among the rest, against the gray sky about to let go its rain.

Another time, the only time I will ever again be so close to a coyote, I was stalking deer amongst the blown downs where they sometimes like to sleep. The place was nearly impenetrable. Cedar trees crisscrossed helter-skelter along the creek bottom. I picked my way through, hopping from grassy hummock to rock to stump to fallen tree, a random course that at times left me looking—instead of for deer—more for a dry place to step. Overhead, the treetops waved in the breeze with the rhythm of a metronome. What a holy silence, a church-like quiet. The woods are so eerie when the skies are gray.

I heard a stick snap, just a little pop, but how the sound resonated in the clarity of the atmosphere, as if ringing across water. Just in front of me a coyote appeared, a ghost flash leaping from the jack pines to stand four-footed on a fallen cedar where he fixed me with his eyes. A grayish dog, flecked with black and yellow, he considered me from a distance that a moment later I would cross with three long strides. At that moment, we traded glances for what seemed like too long, and might have gone on scrutinizing one another for a second or more had I not been so foolish as to try to draw my bow.

In times like these, moving so effortlessly through the woods, oozing around the obstacles in my path like a teardrop of rain sliding down the uneven bark of a tree, I feel like I belong. There is electricity in the air before a storm and a stillness always on the verge of slipping, dropping free, ever so delicately as a drop of dew clinging on the edge of a leaf before it falls.

My first taste of real stillness happened once just before a storm. Sitting along a deer trail still as an owl, I remember that evening on the mountain and how nothing moved, nothing at all, for what seemed like hours. Then a bird—a nuthatch—lit on a nearby branch. Trying to become like rain, I pressed my back into the uneven grooves of the tree while the bird cocked his head, pondering me. I saw a little gleam of light shining in his black, beady eyes, and marveled at how weightless he was an instant later when he hopped down, clutching both feet round my arrow. He pecked once at the wooded shaft, murmured in confusion, then scooted down closer to the broadhead and pecked again before launching himself away in a dipsy flight. I've never felt, though how I've longed for, such stillness ever since.

I come closest to feeling it every winter, the season with the most gray of all. You know that day in autumn, a day leading the hoary edge of winter, when the next storm that comes could bring rain as easily as snow. I try to stop listening to the radioman along about this time out of fear he'll ruin the surprise. My aim is always to be outdoors when the first snowfall of the season comes, to be out of body, drifting through the trees when that magic moment happens and the first flakes glitter down.

Gray days put me in a mood to try drifting through the woods without a sound, to perhaps for a moment feel as light as a nuthatch perched on the tip of an arrow and, maybe, for a little while pretending to be not altogether of this earth. Gray days remind me of how easy it is to disappear for a while and move with a stillness of body and mind that seems effortless when the forest is rapt with silence, when inside you feel enveloped by the clouds.

More than any other time, the woods before a storm reminds

me of poetry and the mystery of what lies out there behind that curtain of mist. I can feel it, and sometimes that's a little frightening. Why? I think the Alaskan poet John Haines said it best, "Out there a flickering pathway leads to a snowy grave where something in me has always wanted to lie."

Rendering the Bones

If the birds are plentiful and I'm shooting well, come November the icebox is stocked with woodcock and ducks and, if I'm shooting *really* well, maybe a few grouse. Each bird, tenderly handled, is drawn and plucked, then wrapped tightly in white freezer paper with cryptic notes scrawled on the outside: little reminders of contents, place, and time.

Drake mallard, The Slough, Long Shot, Opening Day

First Woodcock, The Wagon Wheel Cover, Rainy Saturday

Knowing what I'm eating helps in the remembering of where I've been. But those icy bundles, stacked carefully as bricks, never last as long as the memories. Usually by the end of winter, the wall has crumbled and all I'm left with is a bag of bones.

I save them…"hoard" is a better word. There's a saying around the kitchen that the cook, like the businessman, makes his profits in the margins. That sentiment is at the heart of this recipe, since here it's the essence we're after, every last drop of it.

The French call it a *glace de gibier.* To start, you need an ample amount of onions and what's left after your dinner guests have picked the roasted birdies clean and gone home.

Ingredients are measured by the pinch and fistful. The preparation easily takes the better part of a day. I mention this to warn away those with a need for immediate gratification. Rendering bones takes time.

Unlike a sauce that can cover the taste of a dish, a *glace*, or glaze, heightens the flavor. This one is good over venison and wildfowl, any game really.

What you need:
  15-quart stockpot
  Large frying pan
  Ample amount of yellow onions
  Carcasses of any wild bird left over after cooking
    (Note: I freeze mine in Ziploc bags, storing them
    up until the end of the year.)
  Olive oil
  Bay leaves
  Juniper berries

Start by chopping bones into pieces with a cleaver. The bones of young birds are best, as these contain more gelatin and the marrow contains more flavoring ingredients. Chop a pile of yellow onions equal in size to your pile of bones.

Next, coat your frying pan with olive oil and caramelize the onions (anywhere from 1 to 3 hours depending on quantity), cooking them on a medium heat until they have a soupy consistency and the color of honey.

Lay bones out flat on a cookie sheet and broil 5 minutes, or until they begin to release juices.

Add onions and bones to the stockpot and add water to top off the pot.

Add two bay leaves and a half-dozen juniper berries.

Keep this mixture at a rolling boil, with the lid removed, until half the water has evaporated (from 3 to 4 hours). Then strain the contents through a colander into a bowl, taking care to mash all the liquid from the bones. Pour only the liquid back into the stockpot.

The French define a *glace* as stock reduced to "about a fourth its original volume." So how much stock you have at this stage dictates how much water to add. Add water to the stock in a 3:1 ratio and again bring this to a rolling boil until the water evaporates away and what remains is a deep brown liquid that's noticeably thicker than gravy.

Freeze in plastic containers. For a dinner of four, about one cup will do fine. While warming to serve, add a splash of cognac or some wild morels if you have them.

This year's batch contained the bones of a grouse, a couple of pheasants, a baker's dozen of woodcock, and a wild turkey that almost ran up the pipes of my double-barrel coming into the call. From this, two pots rolling all day on the stove, came about four precious cups of glaze.

Nobody ever understands why I go to all the trouble. It should come as no surprise then that they don't understand the hunting either or, and most importantly, what it means to "suck the marrow out of life." Thoreau may have said it first, but he was only speaking figuratively.

Being There

Hunting might be difficult to discuss in the company of people who don't already understand, but that doesn't stop me from thinking about it. And I think about it a lot, questioning motivation—especially my own—since more often than not I seem to bring home an empty game bag. I'm thinking about the outdoors, the best place I know to ponder such imponderables, yet at the same time how being there has rarely led to any real answers, only more and more inspiration.

I'm hunting around now trying to rout up the right words...

Call it "hope" or, better still, "faith." You don't have to be the church-going kind to know a little something about both. For a certain type of outdoorsman, time passed roving quietly through the woods is practiced with such formality—the act of hunting so ceremonious—and contemplation that the process can stir the soul as deeply as if engaged in some primitive form of prayer.

I'm of a mind that we spend too little time out-of-doors nowadays; I mean actually *being* there. Following paths laid by animals. Deciphering tracks and reading signs. Not just out lollygagging about, merely going through the motions as we so often do every day in our unconscious, habitual lives, but actually moving with purpose in one of the only places left where doing so really matters.

Where else but the woods, while hunting, must we be so conscious of where our feet fall? Where else can a person sit still and listen, essentially doing what most would call nothing, and find so many stirring rewards?

Nowadays, when so many seem to lack humility and patience and so many others seem accustomed to it, I'm glad there are forests and swamps and mountains and wild animals still around to teach us. Likewise for the refuge of hills and valleys—country—where instinct matters more than reason, for all those times this world makes us feel as if we don't belong.

Without the hunt to draw us out, too many people would have no reason to be outdoors. The land is so much more than just pretty scenery, you know. There is something sacred and prayerful about being there when you're really engaged. You feel it every time you're there when the sun breaks through the clouds, behold it in the way the light angles down as if shining through stained glass. You see it in the coyote sulking along a snowy fencerow and in the deer, the buck with ivory-colored antlers that materializes in the shadows right in front of your eyes. You hear it whenever the owl hoots, the raven caws, and a grouse drums its wings somewhere off in the distant pines.

You might think that, because I'm a hunter, you're one kind of person and that I'm another. Maybe you're right if all you see is a bird when you look at a grouse or an animal when you look at a deer.

I see something else...call it "life," one life interconnected; truth, the one truth; and joy, the joy that only a hunter who has been there can know.

A Good Wind

It was the kind of wind that clatters the shutters, tumbles trashcans, and snaps off the tops of tall trees. A hard wind to ignore, cold and angry as all November, that ripped and yowled outside the window that first night and for a handful of days like something dark, dreadful, and awfully upset.

Down at the beach the next morning, a big red sailboat laid upended, its mast splintered and a jagged hole punched in the hull. The neighbor never did find his brand-new Weber grill. Canvasbacks, pintails, and snow geese—migrating fowl seldom seen in these parts and clearly blown off course—were the talk among my duck hunting friends who, like the ducks when those nasty northwinds blow, brave to seek tiny pockets of flat water and the sanctuary of quiet coves.

Hemingway wrote a story about that wind, the "Three Day Blow." Where I live, it happens almost every autumn and, come to think of it, again on the leading edge of spring. A good wind in March, sometimes April, makes for white-capped waves—big, frothy rollers—that pound the beaches north of town. Anglers love it because with the waves come fish, steelhead and brown trout, schooling in shallow from the dark water of Lake Michigan. It's the only time a landlubber can reach them from shore.

Even when I can't fish myself, I sometimes will stop just to watch the others, the surfcasters tending to their long rods buried halfway up the handle in the sand. Something about the wind and the waves and the misty image of a solitary fisherman standing as still as a pier post against the white sky, or wading waist-deep out into the breakers to heave away a long arching cast, strikes me as just about as hopeful and romantic as fishing can get.

While I could do without the leaves and limbs in the yard after a real screamer rips through, I know a good blow in November, a wind that sweeps every bit of fall color from the trees, is simply, as someone once said, how nature clears the deck for winter. Likewise, in springtime, after so many months of snow, a good gale means warm rains are coming, that soon cloudy skies will break and the sun will shine through.

There are popping power lines, uprooted trees, and limbs as big around as your thigh raining down on the roof of the house. Live here long enough and you begin to overlook Mother Nature's blustery tantrums as a matter of course. After all, the wind holds promise. It means change. Up here, the wind brings us game and fish, and it carries the seasons away.

The wind is pretty good company for the rest of the year. Living so close to the big water of Lake Michigan is like living next to the sea; there's always some sort of breeze moving things around. I like a good wind, a steady sea breeze, for flying kites. I like watching the crows dip and dive on a headwind high over the green pastures and the way a sudden gust can raise a cat's paws on a quiet pond (it looks like minnows dancing, splashing on the top like a handful of shot tossed on the water, away from the jaws of something hungry down below).

I never tire of listening to the wind. It carries the tinkling of chimes and, in springtime and at night across the lake, makes the bonfire conversations of distant neighbors sound so close we might as well be sharing the same camp. I like the way the wind smells up here, on some nights like grass clippings and cherry blossoms and pine. I like how, just before a rain shower, a good wind turns up the pale underbellies of summertime leaves, flashing a warning that a storm is coming so it's time to head inside.

When it comes right down to it, I guess what I'm getting at is that, best of all, I like the way a good wind can sometimes move me and, in a manner of speaking, fill my sails.

Just the other day, walking along the beach at sunset, my wife walking up ahead and tossing a stick into the big waves for the dogs, the wind came along, a shore breeze blowing west down from the piney hills and over the water toward the skyline. We had had words earlier that day, one of those pointless disagreements about something of little bearing, followed by a long, uncomfortably quiet drive to the beach. I don't remember the details, only the wind that blew away any recollection of the harsh words muttered between us as I watched it ever so gently tossing the hair of the one I love.

Belly Boats and Backwaters

A loon told me the lake was there. It was not on any map.

The first pond, at a glance a wonderful little fishing hole (but not the one I want to tell you about), caught my eye every day on the way to work. No road or two-track led back to it. The sliver of tea-colored water I could see appeared far enough into the trees that, with so many more easily accessible lakes nearby, a place like this was surely one not fished very often.

Living in northern Michigan, I have become an aficionado of small water such as this—or rather, those places often overlooked by locals and visiting tourists in the hustle of summertime. With so much storied water in these parts, a good fishing hole doesn't always have to be out-of-the-way. More famous water acts as the perfect diversion.

For instance, a couple of miles from my house is the lake where the reigning state-record bluegill was caught. Another was once home to the biggest musky. Still another is so renowned for its walleye fishing that I once met two men at the boat dock who had driven all the way from Georgia after reading about the place in a national fishing magazine.

At first glance, this particular roadside pond had the look of a bluegill spot. A quick check of the topographical map showed a tiny nameless fleck of blue surrounded by land that was every bit public. But what interested me more was the squiggly blue hairline that indicated a stream, one that connected the pond to another, and still another, further in. Further usually meaning better, I took a pencil and circled the last.

What angler doesn't daydream of discovering secret water and casting to fish that have never seen a fly before? Secluded water, well off the beaten path, usually means big fish, lots of fish. A fisherman's paradise. Sure, it's an experience just "being there," finding a bit of water to call your own for an afternoon. But to fully realize the magic of secluded water, you need to catch some fish. You need to fish the place effectively.

When my back wasn't giving me fits and great fishing was the goal, no distance was too far to carry my canoe. No doubt, my lousy posture is partly due to the insane miles bushwhacked carrying such burdensome loads.

An out-of-the-way fishing hole is usually one surrounded by brushy banks not trampled by footpaths. My favorite places are beaver ponds, new ones, where the silt and mud hasn't yet had time to collect and conspire to do in any trout that might be living there.

Beavers, as adept as they are at damming a stream, could care less about trimming back the brush at the water's edge. Without a canoe, I was forced to fish these places from shore. That's fine for those times when I was drowning worms with spin gear. But these days, I like fishing with my fly rod. Unfortunately, brush-choked banks make a good backcast utterly impossible.

So inspired by the glam and glitzy photos of fly fishermen high atop those treeless slopes in the West, alone in the solitude of some forgotten alpine lake, I took a payment I'd have otherwise made to the chiropractor and bought myself a float tube.

Coming upon that second pond was like stumbling onto buried treasure. I followed the stream inland, a winding course between high, fern-covered banks and sun-washed green meadows. A dark cedar swamp, the trees and their great gnarled trunks like witch's fingers poking up through the ground, reminded me of a scene from a fairy tale.

The slough was much smaller than I'd envisioned, shaped like a kidney bean, and surrounded by bog. I was surrounded by more crooked trees, black and jagged against the sky, and a maddening swarm of mosquitoes that had followed me in from the road.

My map was obviously old. What was once water was no longer. You could chuck a stone into the cattails on the far bank of the pond.

Undaunted, I crept to the water's edge, parted the tall grass, and saw cruising the edge of the lily pads a dozen or so coffee-saucer sized bluegills and a few tiny bass. Instead of darting away, when I stepped into the open, more fish—one bass of a pound or two, came in for a closer look. A turkey shoot, I thought.

The small white popper picked off a dozen fish in a dozen casts: bass and bluegill both, but nothing of any size. A bigger fly was in order, perhaps something that resembled a small bird or a frog. I tied on a deer hair imitation of the latter, a startlingly realistic green and yellow creation with long straw legs that dangled down deliciously.

I slapped this on the water close to the edge of the lily pads and stripped it back with a series of snappy tugs. The frog sounded a *ka-chunk...ka-chunk...ka-chunk*—a dinner bell to a hungry bass—as it cut a frantic V-wake back toward me through the water.

When the schools of smaller fishes attacked, it turned the water into a froth, knocking the gargantuan froggy clean out of the water on occasion. But after an hour's worth of casting that took me around the entire perimeter of the pond, I only managed to land one bass with a mouth big enough to inhale my offering.

The fish in this pond were stunted, every one a mirror image of the next. It's a condition common to deserted waterways—a wonderful case *against* the practice of "catch-and-release"; without fishermen taking a few for the table, the only limiting factor for the fish is old age and predation by the occasional snapping turtle or blue heron.

I don't typically keep fish. But I often make exception when it comes to bluegills, their crispy flesh fried golden in oil in a cast-iron skillet. When it comes to panfish, to hell with what's prim and proper. I say, "Please, pass the salt." Especially in this instance, where you didn't need a degree in marine biology to see this pond needed a good culling.

I fished here, secretly, a half-dozen times before I heard the loon cry from beyond the trees. There wasn't much thought wasted on the meaning of it. On the west end of the pond, I had fished the mouth of the tiny creek that trickled over a bed of milfoil. The creek came from somewhere, I just didn't know from where.

So shouldering my tube and daypack, I blazed a trail through the cattails, high-steeping the deadfalls, ducking cedar boughs, and twice stepping into mud holes that covered my waders up to the waist with that foul smelling, black-swamp goop.

The lake was crescent-shaped, flat calm. My first thought was that if a big bass existed anywhere on this earth, surely the gentle hand of God placed one in this heavenly place. The greenest of hills grew up from the water, surrounding it. A dozen or so fish were making rings along the edge. I heard the *pop, pop, pop* of bluegills kissing the bottom of the lily pads. I stood agog as a brace of mallards leapt suddenly into the air and the loon called again as if on some cosmic cue.

For my fly selection, I went conservative at first, forgoing the biggest bass bugs in my box for something more subdued. A Yuk Bug, one of my favorite flies, proved good for two palm-sized bluegills.

Like curious onlookers, the bluegills and sunfish encircled my belly boat by the dozens. A few made daring assaults to the tube's underbelly. They pecked at my fins, then hovered there with fish lips gaping.

The water was crystal. Twenty feet below, I saw dark shadows cruising the bottom. Bass, I thought. Hogs. Kicking my way over to a fallen tree, its tangled crown half-submerged under water, I dropped the bug in soft and tight. It made a dimple on the surface and another bluegill was tight on the line.

What happened next is the fodder for a fish tale. A shadow, nearly an arm's length, came from below, rolled at the surface, and flashed white. What I thought was a pike jumped clear of the surface after a surging run. It was a bass, green-sided, with a pale round underbelly as big as a grapefruit.

The bluegill rocketed skyward from his cavernous mouth like it was shot from a Roman candle. Thinking the bluegill was surely dead, I reeled in the tiny fish. His sides showed creases where the bass had held him. Seemingly none the worse for wear, he darted away when I placed him back in the water.

It was the stuff of dreams. I had heard of bass like these, bloodthirsty carnivores that lurked in the shadows and dined regularly on bullfrogs, baby ducklings, and water snakes. I won't tell you I hooked him on the very next cast, or even that day. But I did the next day after tearing off to the fly shop early in the morning and buying two of the biggest bass flies I've ever seen. They weren't really flies at all. More like the maker had simply taken an entire deer tail and lashed two pheasant wings to it with a spool of sparkling line.

After carefully finding my way into striking distance, I heaved the monstrosity to the water and it hit like a stone. There was neither a moment's hesitation nor an instant to rethink the cast. The fish struck and struck hard. What I remember after that was a surging run for the middle of the lake, the heavy orange fly line ripping the water behind him in a shallow arch. He ran deep, a muddy streak boiling in his wake.

I have only vague recognition of what happened next, how the line came to a sickening halt, snagged in the milfoil and grass on the bottom, how when I frantically kicked over to where the water bubbled, an apparition of the fish appeared on the bottom, hopelessly tangled.

Then a voice, like being roused from a dream, "Whatta ya got?"

I looked around, dazed, and there on the bank stood a man. I was close enough to read the writing on his t-shirt, "WOMEN WANT ME. FISH FEAR ME."

He laughed and spit when I told him how far I'd walked, pointed up the hill behind him where his truck was parked, and said something about the main road, a two-track, how him and few buddies come here to "throw back a couple cold ones" all the time.

The bass was gone. And I didn't feel much like fishing after that.

I've fished here many times since, every time alone. As far as fishing holes go, it remains one of the most secluded, one of the best, I've ever "discovered." With the road so close, it's not quite the secret spot I'd first thought it to be. But some days, bobbing alone out there in the middle, I can muster the feelings I had when I first happened upon it. It is as if this place is paradise once again. And my float tube…the magic carpet that brought me here.

Letter of Apology to My Neighbor: The Squirrel Sympathizer

It's fall and the squirrels are running amuck in our rustic and otherwise homey little subdivision. Black squirrels. Gray squirrels. Red squirrels. Flying squirrels. The only thing worse than having squirrels taking over your yard and bird feeders, not to mention shacking up in your attic, is having neighbors who sympathize with the enemy.

I might as well just come out and say it: There was a huge misunderstanding with the neighbor. I felt wrongly accused. Still, the Mrs. says *I* should be the one to apologize. So here goes. I'm giving it my best shot.

> My Dear Neighbor,
>
> Because I don't believe that harboring anger or animosity toward your neighbors is a good thing, let me first apologize for my end of the misunderstanding we had this morning regarding the subject of urban squirrel management. I also apologize for that deceased squirrel you found on your property last fall (though, as I said this morning, I rarely ever pull a shot and thus suspect it a casualty of the road).

You mentioned the hunting season on squirrels, how you're pretty sure that what you wrongly believe I did—and for that matter what you believe I am doing— is against the law. Well, I feel compelled to kindly offer that, in fact, when it comes to squirrels, the state is actually quite generous with bag limits allowing gunning from October to March. Not that it matters, since state game regulations—when it comes to the handling of varmints and pests responsible for the destruction of private property—are essentially suspended.

You may love the squirrels, and I must offer that I do as well, provided the little troublemakers stick to their side of the treeline. Not when they destroy in one month's time two bird feeders I purchased for around $60 total. Likewise, when on two separate occasions, squirrels have chewed their way into the attic space of my home. At that point, the squirrel becomes no better, no worse, than the moles digging up my yard, the rabbit munching the carrots in my victory garden, the chipmunk that chewed his way into my garage, or the mice that decide to winter in my $350 pair of Gore-Tex fishing waders, gnawing a drafty, fist-sized front door right through the rear end in the process.

As a homeowner, I reserve the right to protect my residence and property from these pesky interlopers, provided, by law, the means does not put at risk of injury or bodily harm any neighbors and/or innocent bystanders.

Please know that in respecting your earlier request, I no longer "hurt the squirrels" and have not used any lethal means on my property since your last visit (the duo of late-night rabblerousing squirrels that decided to take up residence in the attic this past fall notwithstanding). Instead, I have merely tried to dissuade them from destroying the $90 feeder I have hung in the yard (the advertisement promised "squirrel proof," but, alas, it is not).

Obviously, encouraging them back into the happy sanctuary of your yard with a child's slingshot—a highly inaccurate, ineffective thing—is also not acceptable to you. In the interest of preventing further unrest, and possible sleepless nights, you have my promise that I will cease and desist with that undertaking as well. Even though it's an option, I am not particularly fond of rat poison; it makes my favorite fricassee inedible and would likewise result in a scurry of squirrels turning up dead around your little goldfish pond. Now, maybe I'll have to reevaluate that.

Even though I've been told it's a pipedream, I suspect that in the end, the man or woman who finally comes up with a totally fail-safe way to squirrel-proof a yard and home will be blessed with untold riches. Rest assured, given our sluggish economy and my profession as a writer, I will have ample time to try.

At any rate, I'm sorry again that we seem to have a philosophical difference when it comes to the squirrels. But on that, we will simply have to agree to disagree. I will now consider this issue in the past as I hope you will as well.

Respectfully,
Bob

Getting Away From It All

L et's go camping.

No three words short of "Amount Past Due" so often conspire to fill me with more dread. Chalk it up to what qualifies as camping in people's minds these days, including my wife's. Just park it and pitch it and *viola!* She thinks we're roughing it.

You'll have to excuse the bad mood. At Nancy's behest, we went camping this weekend. Or called it that. Before I go any further, you should understand that I don't dislike all kinds of camping, just the sort that puts me in close proximately to other humans. I also don't like the fact that, come summer, the woods up here are crawling with out-of-towners that make a little wilderness peace and quiet virtually impossible. Consider this: If your destination is northern Michigan and you intend to pitch a tent in one of our designated campgrounds, the forest service advises booking your spot well in advance. You get no preference points for living here, which is why we ended up on the river.

My idea of getting away from it all starts when you weigh your backpack in ounces rather than pounds, sometimes forgoing comforts such as a tent, a sleeping bag, food, and water if the distance from the trailhead demands it. Hell, I've even hacked off the end of my toothbrush just to save my bum knee the burden of a single unnecessary ounce.

But I love my wife, so in the interest of compromise, did my part to come up with a plan that on paper seemed to suit us both: two days of canoeing and one night spent camping on the riverbank under the stars. The upper reaches of the river were unknown to us. The map revealed nothing but glorious swamp for dozens of miles along our windy route. When you're camping out of a canoe, you can't help but pack light. But then part of the fun in camping, at least to my way of thinking, is in taking a vacation from convenience. Isn't to deprive oneself of comfort the best way to learn to appreciate it more?

A guidebook of the area used words like "undeveloped" and "uninhabited" to describe the countryside through which we would be floating. There was also a mention of campgrounds—one for car campers and one for canoeists—that I would have rather avoided altogether. But the canoeist's campground was delightfully described as "a primitive facility." Further, the phrase "walk-in only" suggested to me the possibility of peace, while for my wife the promise of running water and a commode.

If there is anything that can ruin the tranquility of a river faster than a canoe livery, I can't think of it at the moment. Come to find a busy one was situated right along the highway at the take-out. The vans, running in tandem, towing rattling trailers stacked high with aluminum canoes, were packed with happy day-trippers squeezed together four and five on a seat. Nancy and I would put-in much farther up river than they. And that part of the trip was divine.

We saw cedar waxwings, kingfishers, and blue herons. We rounded a bend and saw a deer standing in the river, trout sucking insects, a happy muskrat swimming under the canoe. The sun was so warm. The breeze smelled of summer. Then we heard the screams.

Am I the only one who thinks a river ought not to be treated like a water fun-park? Am I out of line suggesting I'd rather hear birdsong outdoors than the hoots and hollers from some half-crocked, lobster-fried canoers and tubers alternately sipping from their two-fisted cans? Why am I the only one who doesn't think it's cute or funny, not in the least, when some bratty kid sitting in ambush on the bank tries to shoot me in the head with his Super Soaker™?

The campground was even worse. Not another canoe-camper in the place. In forest service speak, "walk-in" translated into an easy saunter from the parking lot, where the engines of muscle cars rumbled away the afternoon, announcing the comings and goings of underage teens.

The place was crawling with them. By the looks of the tent city they erected, it was obvious they intended to stay. Down by the river, a rowdy bunch organized, armed with more Super Soakers™ of their own. For an hour or so, any canoer passing through had to run their little gauntlet until finally this beefy, bearded trucker-looking guy loudly proclaimed that if one drop of water touched him, the shooters could look forward to having one of those mega hydro-cannons firmly ensconced in their kiesters...or words to that effect.

All this happened and more. Further, since this was a Forest Service campground, we actually had to pay for the privilege of staying here. After depositing our money in the little envelope slot, we walked past a group of kids huddled under a cedar tree sucking suds through a tube and funnel.

"Hey dude," one of them hollered to me, "want a beer-bong?"

Ah, the venerable beer-bong. What could be more refreshing after a day spent on the river in the great outdoors? I was touched by the offer. But alas, I had to pass.

Come nightfall those crazy kids started dancing around the campfire and howling at the moon. So this story could go on, but once again, I'm out of space. Perhaps the next time I go searching for a little peace and quiet, I think I'll save myself the packing and simply stay at home.

The Dogman

A couple of campfires ago, in the darkest hours between midnight and dawn, a drift of us were sitting around caveman-style in a merry discussion about trout. There we sat, passing the last of the cider, when from down by the river came a noise like claws scraping metal. A beat of unnerving silence followed as we sat, open-mouthed and gawping saucer-eyed at one another, until there came the unmistakable clamor of a 17-foot Grumman canoe being wrapped like a bowtie around a birch tree.

"What the hell was that?" The words squeaked from my throat. Somebody had already grabbed the frying pan and dove for the nearest tent, leaving me and the last man knocking heads when both of us bent over to select just the right stone for bashing in the killer's skull.

Eventually we three stooges summoned our courage enough to whisper a plan. The three of us would talk our way down to the river's edge using angry and pretend voices, the idea being that it was better to sound like a mob of very ornery, torch-wielding villagers instead of the crap-in-the-pants fishermen we were.

Near as we could tell, it was probably a raccoon, or maybe just the wind. We had some groceries down there chilling in shallow river water. Or maybe the canoe and the rods left propped up against a tree had simply toppled over. Nobody really believed it was the Dogman, which has to be the strangest ghost story still in frequent campfire rotation up here.

According to the legend, in the late seventeenth century, a band of French trappers ventured up river, deep into the unbroken forests then known only as the land of the Chippewa, now the northern Lower Peninsula. They had the white man's first run-in with a beast they described as a "la loup garou," a werewolf. All but two of the French men had retired early that night, leaving the pair alone to keep a lookout and to tend to the campfire until dawn. A couple of hours later, the wood pile running low, one of the men went off into the forest looking for more to burn when—Sacre bleu!—in the light of the full moon, a wild dog appeared on the trail. The Dogman rose up. The Frenchie pulled a knife. In the ensuing struggle the part-dog-part-man whatchamacallit lunged for the trapper's throat but with one deft move of the blade, the Frenchmen slashed the monster's ear clean off, sending it screaming into the night.

Hurrying back to camp, the man became lost, wandering in circles until the morning. With his clothing torn and bloody, the trapper, probably babbling incoherently and wielding his knife, busted through the undergrowth and collapsed before a line of ghostly faces staring down the pipes of their muskets cocked and ready to fire. Leading the fire squad was the second man from the fire the night before, his head wrapped in a bandage wet with a deep crimson stain over where the ear should have been.

Years later, in 1887, at a lumber camp in Wexford County along the Manistee River, one evening a group of loggers happened upon a huge wild dog in the forest. They cornered the animal and upon clobbering it with a stick, the monster stood and came forth with a horrible man-like scream. The story goes that every logger's hair turned white and their faces stayed ashen with fear for the rest of their days.

There's the story of an old farmer in Buckley who, after working into the night under a bright harvest moon, was found slumped over his plow the next morning; reportedly died from fright. Strange tracks, like a man's feet but hairy and with claws, were all around the body. The same tracks were found in 1906 after an old widow confided to friends about nightmares she was having in which a pack of dogs that howled at the moon with human screams tried to get in her home. Townsfolk later found her dead of a heart attack, a ghoulish expression of fear on her face, and the tracks of the Dogman pressed in the snow outside her open window.

Less than a quarter century ago, a Cadillac raccoon hunter named Fortney got a good look at the Dogman running with a pack of what appeared to be wild dogs. Fearing for his skin, Fortney fired a shot into the air, only to be struck dumb when from the middle of the rout something man-like and covered with hair stood up on two legs and reportedly "sneered" at him before vanishing into the dark.

And so the legend goes. Back at the campfire, after we righted the rods and canoe, bagged what remained of our grub, and hung the sack in a tree, the Dogman bore out other unbelievable tales of Bigfoot, poltergeists, black panthers, and UFOs. Up in Michigan, we have more than our fair share of those occurrences, too. While I don't know what it all means exactly, what I like to remember is that, while we laughed at some of the stories, we nodded knowingly at others, and that before we knew it, dawn had come and it was time to go home where we all could at last feel invincible once again.

Dream Fish, Night Fish

In September, when the great schools of salmon start nosing
upstream en masse to their dying places, the riverside mayhem of
crazed anglers that ensues hardly qualifies as fishing. What drives
fishermen to unruly, often illegal, acts? Perhaps it's simply the vexing
vision of water black with multitudes of enormous fish, every one
of which steadfastly refuses to strike at anything offered. Or maybe
autumn's cold bite awakens some dormant survival instinct in some
humans that make us mad for wild food; maybe it's the knowledge
that winter is on the way and their larder is unstocked. Or perhaps
what boils the angler's blood is the understanding that, unless
caught, all that precious meat fining in the shallows is destined to
rot and go to waste.

Whatever it is, salmon bring out the animal in people.

You see it at all the popular places fishermen gather, the river
holes where the fish stack up like cordwood in the current. Here
the masses toss random obscenities at both fish and fellow anglers.
Occasionally fistfights break out. It starts when somebody hollers,
"Fish On!" and the salmon makes its first, surging run, invariably
crisscrossing a dozen other lines in the process that, once impossibly
tangled, begin popping like .22 shots.

Such a commotion spooks the skittish salmon. They are already wary of shadows on the bank, not to mention the shower of lead sinkers and lures raining down. I shy away from the daytime chaos that accompanies fishing the fall salmon run. Looking for quiet, I do most of salmon fishing at night.

Fishing, at its best, is done on faith; alone, or maybe with a friend you fix to meet up with a few bends downstream. The faith comes in believing that the dark pools, cut banks, and sunken logs hide fish. But you'll never actually see them until the silver-flash that precedes the wallop of the strike.

Fishing at its best is also done by feel. After dark, that's all there is.

I most like fishing for salmon at the river's mouth, where you stand in water up to your armpits. There, under the wide eyes of the moon, in the near dark, I tie my knots by feel, by memory.

With any fish but salmon, I prefer delicate tackle, tiny hand-tied flies, and long rods as sensitive as nerve endings. But on these nights, I come wanting a good fight and, admittedly, meat that—out here in the dark—seems more fairly won.

Good faith is not easily held. I sometimes cast at nothing for hours—long arching casts that play out over the water and disappear with a plop. Then count:

*One-one-thousand…two-one-thousand…*every second the lure drops another foot down.

I count until the spoon sinks five, maybe six feet.

Behind me, the waves roll up on the beach like a heartbeat, slow and narcotic. The water presses against my thighs. I try to imagine what the lure looks like down there, flashing in the moonlight with every twitch of the rod. I imagine it—a wounded minnow—wobbling and falling past schools of silver salmon, hoping for that one fish that strikes out of anger, a white-hot flash of frustration. Who knows, perhaps he's even as hungry as I am.

Whatever the reason, when one strikes, there's no mistaking it—not out here where there are no rocks, no limbs, no beer cans to snag. The fish hits like a sledge and I awaken as if from a trance, heaving backward, the rod bent in two and the line tight as piano wire.

Also, I feel as if I've cast into rush hour traffic and snagged the back bumper of a pickup. The initial hit is that wrenching. If it's a big salmon, the instant a salmon hits can be the most crucial time. It is in this moment of unreadiness that the fish is liable to break water, throw the hook, or snap free.

Fishermen often compare big fish to dreams, and at this instant, I understand why. This one pulls steadily away as I struggle to gain line, to hang on, realizing all the while that, like a dream, the magic is slipping away and perhaps might never get this good again.

The Lights of Downtown L.A.

During the months Nancy was expecting, one of the things people said repeatedly was how much babies make a person look at the world...*differently*. That and how I should make sure to enjoy it while I could because the time really will go by in a flash.

Well, Gabe arrived in September and the next thing I knew it was February—just like that. Five months. Days and weeks just gone, vanished in a proverbial *Poof!* Deep in a zombie-like unconsciousness state more commonly known as "new fatherhood," I realized that—yes—it really was all going by in a blur if by "it" you mean what was left of my life.

One day I seriously started to wonder: Was this finally the punch line to an inside joke?

After bringing the baby home, my wife and I didn't get out much. Ten weeks later, she went back to work, leaving me home alone with the boy, and between the rocking and the swaddling, the doctor visits, the grocery shopping, the bottle feedings every two hours on the hour...I didn't get out at all. No more blowing off a deadline to go frolic with the fishes. Forget about disappearing "out there" for even just an hour, let alone the devil-may-care days when I used to ditch my cell phone and wristwatch on the counter and spend the entire day chasing grouse and woodcock out in the sunny aspens with the dogs.

Therefore, I really did start looking at the world differently. It started soon after I finally figured the best way to get some sleep was to nap during the day when the baby did. Only this led to keeping strange hours…night hours.

Mostly, I wrote when the house was dark and quiet. But it was not good writing. Gabe slept in the room across the hall from my office where I raced against the clock for two, maybe three-hour intervals with the five-fingered fury of a man trying to defuse a bomb.

With my ear subconsciously pricked for the slightest whimper or restless groan (the indication that the baby was about to blow), my stories came out all disjointed and hurried, mirroring my thoughts.

Outside the office, things weren't going much better. A friend called to say he saw me tearing through the grocery store, giggling and singing Christmas carols to the baby kicking and cooing in the cart. It was February, a foot of snow outside, and I was wearing flip-flops. My hair had grown wild and long and the message on the machine said I sort of looked out-of-it—"deranged," he said—like one of those people who spend all day in their bathrobe and fuzzy slippers listening to AM radio and penning angry letters to the local newspaper editor.

One day even Nancy, home from a business trip, voiced concern.

"You should get out. Do something," she said. "At least go for a walk."

So I took a sundown stroll through the neighborhood, but it felt odd walking the streets alone. Dogs barked at me. Neighbors I didn't have the time to meet looked up from their snow shoveling with suspicious glances.

So I started going out well after dark, a little later every time. Idly peering in people's windows as they ate dinner and lounged on the couch watching the news, I felt like the character in Robert Frost's poem "Acquainted with the Night." Frost had always been a favorite of mine, particularly after I realized that he had four kids in the house about the same time he wrote that one, which means, as a man and a poet, he was probably worse off than I.

Then in February, three o'clock in the morning, cold, dark, and lightly snowing, the boy was asleep (finally and again) and I found myself frantically digging in the closest for my fur hat and woolens. I grabbed my snowshoes and crept into the bedroom where Nancy was asleep and whispered that for the next couple of hours she was on deck. I was going for my walk. Only this time I headed for the woods.

One of the reasons we moved to Lake Ann was to be near the woods. When I drove through what constitutes town—lovely downtown L.A.—the only things moving were the snowflakes swirling in the headlights, like dust after a nuclear blast.

The trailhead parking lot was empty, too, when I struck off through the woods down the trail. No flashlight for me, just the blue-gray light of a big full moon reflecting off the snow.

In the forest on a cold night, the stumps and bushes took on the shapes of lurking animals. Trees popped and growled. Suddenly I was afraid, a genuine fear stirring in the back of my brain, not because of the unwelcoming darkness, but from another concern manifesting in my brain.

When I was at home, all I could think about was getting away to the woods, miles away, if only for an hour to walk aimlessly alone breathing fresh air un-tinged by the smell of Johnson's Baby Powder® and Desitin®. Now that I was here, the real joke finally hit me. Now all I could think about was home.

As I slogged through the knee-high snow, I felt weak and pathetic, cold, my chest hollow and empty. I walked faster until the lake appeared at the bottom of the hill, frozen over, a sheet of white, and through the fog on the other side, the town—a cluster of hazy street and porch lights—our town. I stood there for I don't know how long, just watching, trying to feel…something, anything, all the time thinking "what the hell is happening to me?"

The lights looked like tiny stars or fireflies stuck on glow, like little campfires in the dark woods along the far shore. I thought of the baby sleeping, Nancy waking and finding the driveway minus one car. Just like that, I turned away from the lights, away from the long loop trail through the woods, making a new path through the darkness that might find me the shortest route home.

A String and a Prayer

It was nearing the end of the session. Time to find my quiet place. "Close your eyes and breathe," she said. "Just *breeeeathe*." Well, okay. A pond. I conjured the image of a pond. A glittering jewel of green water lined with lily pads and cattails, happy white birch trees and towering pines.

"Now picture the ocean," she said.

I opened an eye.

"The what?"

"Today I want you to try to imagine the open sea. And a boat. A boat big enough to carry all your troubles away."

How about the *Queen Mary*, I thought, picturing the great ship tugging out of the harbor with the good doctor, a tiny speck, waving bye-bye from way up high behind the white rails of the airy open deck. I know she meant well, but for weeks we'd been doing this little guided exercise the same way. I liked my pond and told her so.

She sort of smirked and made a noise, "Haa!," like a mallard duck. Then she took a note.

Okay, so maybe I did have a problem with being able to just let go. In hindsight, I chalk it up to too much work and not enough fishing. It really does make Bob a dull boy. There's an old saying that if people concentrated on the really important things in life, there would be a shortage of fishing poles. Such is the long way around getting to the point of this little story. Who needs imaginary boats to carry away the stresses of living when you have bobbers and bluegill ponds?

Where fishing is concerned, I'm finding that the older I get, the more inclined I am to practice the endeavor in its most elemental form; that is, with a simple hook and a line.

I like the smell of this kind of fishing, which to me is the fragrance of coffee grounds and potting soil. Worms. For years, I considered myself a fly fisherman. In doing so, I forgot the delightful terror I used to feel when reaching my fingers into a bait bucket full of pinching crayfish. I forgot how much I used to enjoy digging in the earth for worms.

When I was small, my father and I would prepare for a weekend fishing trip days in advance. I was the only kid I knew who actually used to pray for rain, a good summer downpour to soak the backyard. Come nightfall, my father would operate the flashlight as I crept barefoot beside him through the dewy grass, pinching up nightcrawlers, one after the other.

Looking back on it now, the most vivid memories I have of fishing with my dad come not from the actual fishing, but rather from when the two of us would head off into the night to rustle up some bait. That or striking off across the field to the creek in the hollow behind our house, a place just loaded with minnows and crayfish. Going there to catch bait was itself an adventure.

We used to put on our old sneakers and roll up our pant legs. My father would set up with his minnow seine spanning a narrow place while I went upstream to wait for his signal. When he'd holler, "Ready!," I came on down like a moose, sloshing and splashing, kicking around and plunging headlong into the deeper holes, pushing the minnows out ahead of me. It was rare to come around the bend and not find my dad heaving up what seemed like hundreds of fat, pale-belly chubs, daces, and red darters.

For a boy of seven, it was marvelously muddy and rewarding work—almost as much fun as the actual fishing. Even the time I crawled out of the creek and went to wipe off my legs what I thought was leafy debris. Only they weren't little black leaves stuck to my shins...they were leeches and a good number of them, too. I tried pulling one off me and, finding it stuck fast, was filled with a sinking and woozy sense of imminent doom. Men in funny pith helmets and safari shorts were often getting in trouble with leeches in the Africa I knew from watching *Tarzan*, my favorite after-school television show at the time. I kept thinking that any moment I, too, would start flailing on the bank and tearing at my clothes until rendered weak and unconscious by sweet, blood-sucking death.

My father, however, not only remained calm, he was beaming with a Eureka-like smile. Leeches, it turned out, were a godsend. As I sat in the mud feeling sick, he carefully plucked the leeches away one by one, dropping each into the bait bucket where they coiled and squirmed in the water like little, black, sinister-looking eels.

"Good work, son," he said, tossing my hair. "Those are some beauties you got there."

I ended up landing one of the biggest bass in my life that day on one of those leeches. It was the only fish of the day. First my bobber, a little plastic red and white job, was there and then it was not. I reared back on the rod and the fish's head broke water like a nuclear sub. A shower of white foam and a flash of red gills and a gaping mouth that looked as big as the open end of a garbage can. Fish like that have a way of teaching you a thing or two about keeping sight of your priorities. After that, I never got queasy about leeches latching onto my flesh again. I also learned to not lose focus, to not lose hope, even after hours of sitting in the hot sun waiting for a fish to strike.

In fact, where physical discomfort is concerned, I discovered that in the process of fishing, the degree of sunburn, windburn, general all-round nastiness, and/or downright boredom I could endure was often directly proportionate to any good fishing fortune that might chance to come along and gobble up the wiggling bit of bait at the end of my line. Fishing taught me that good luck was the stuff that came about through patience and persistence. Good luck, I also determined, was often created through the good work that often preceded it.

I'm only thirty-four, too young to be sounding like a grizzly old curmudgeon, but when I look around at the kids today (and, come to think of it, a lot of adults, too) I can tell almost at a glance the ones who make time for fishing and the ones who don't.

The kids in my neighborhood who fish strike me as a determined lot. They all have good healthy suntans. I see them nearly every day in the summertime, riding their bikes at a good clip down the dirt road that leads to a great little bass and bluegill pond in the woods. Fishing there myself one day, I was struck at how quiet, how dogged they were, even when that afternoon nothing was biting except the deer flies and mosquitoes.

These two little boys, wearing baseball caps pulled low, stood like silent Indians on the bank. They never once took their eyes off the water, never strayed more than an arm's reach away from the pair of Y-shaped sticks where they carefully rested their fishing rods while waiting for a strike. Somehow I doubt children like these are among the herky-jerky horde of delinquents you hear about so often on the news. I like to think that they are also the kids who grow up to be the kind of adults who not only don't mind a little dirt under their fingernails, but who also never gaze down at their hands at the end of the day wondering what they did with the hours.

When I think of how fishing enables a person to just kick back and relax, to get back in touch with family and oneself, about the only problem I can see with fishing is that many people who would benefit from the perspective angling offers never think to give it a try.

On days when things just aren't going right, times when I feel put out and put upon, I find myself longing for a quiet place on the water. I daydream about my own personal paradise, a pond, and me sitting at the end of a wooden dock with a fishing pole and a bucket full of bait. Fishing for me is a soothing combination of contemplation and concentration. When my eyes are drawn down to a single spot on the water—the bobber starts to pop and twitch and then suddenly disappears—everything else around it turns fuzzy. Any feeling of disconnectedness disappears with the widening ripples and for a moment, I feel attached, literally by an invisible thread, to something out there really *alive*. It's the best therapy I know.

Fishing with the Boy

Of all the things people told me to expect from new fatherhood, nobody mentioned anything about the fishing—at least, nothing good. Little babies and fishing don't mix was the unsettling consensus among my angling friends. That and the fact that, overall, life as I knew it was pretty much over.

"Butzie! Call me. Just wanted to see how much you'd take for that little Loomis rig. Heard you're having a kid and figured—Har-Har—you sure as heck won't need it anymore."

Leading up to the magic month of September—or D-Day as one of my friends had taken to calling Nancy's delivery date—the only trouble I had with all the good-natured ribbing and occasional gaff on the message machine was that some of my buddies are fishing fathers who were actually speaking from experience.

It was true. The spring after Gabe was born, I didn't hit the river half as much as before. But a funny thing happened: I didn't much miss it.

There, I said it.

Suddenly, trout seemed, well, trivial. I was a Dad with a capital "D." No time for standing in water up to my butt waving a stick over my head. No money to spare for new fly line and flies.

I was so into fly-fishing I occasionally wrote about it. I used to hit the river decked out in all the latest gear, looking so downright hip and fashionable that I occasionally saw my picture in popular outdoor magazines. This brings to mind another running joke from those who've actually seen me out there, madly whipping the water into a frenzied froth…"You know, Butzman, a couple casting lessons would cost you less than what you dropped on those new Gore-Tex waders."

Fair enough.

Those few times I did get to fish that first year, I spent most of my time just sitting, collapsed on the bank, cock-eyed, staring at fish rising all around me with what combat veterans call the thousand-yard stare. I became a haggard-looking thirty-something guy in leaky waders patched with duct tape. Too whipped even to slap at the mosquitoes, I entertained strange, sleep-deprived thoughts. One day, for instance, I found myself wondering long and hard if anyone has ever been sucked totally to death by mosquitoes and, if not, hoped maybe I might be the first.

Another evening, I cast and cast to a rising brown until my designated hour was up and only then realized I had forgotten to actually tie on a fly. Shedding my gear and racing back home to relieve my lovely, understanding, and infinitely patient wife, I charged in the house with what looked like a giant pee-stain on my pants. Over the winter, a chipmunk seeking handier access to his cache of winter nuts decided to chew a formidable hole in the nether regions of my waders and my patch job was sub par.

"Great," Nancy said. "Do we have to start buying diapers for you now? It looks like you wet yourself out there."

It wasn't that I didn't have the energy for a retort. In my postpartum funk (not just for women anymore), the truth was that I actually had to wonder for a moment if it really was just river water.

When people tell you parenthood is a "real life changer," it's typically with a wide-eyed, better-you-than-me look of pity before they give you that line about it being hard in the beginning but how, eventually, it gets much better. For me it started to change one day in the sporting goods aisle of our local Meijer store. I was browsing plastic bobbers and purple plastic worms when I was supposed to be picking up another pallet of Huggies destined for the neighborhood landfill.

Into the cart went the salve, the baby wash, Gabe's "appy juice" (apple juice), and a half-gallon of that special, sweet amber "happy juice" that makes the parental machine run (scotch—blended, of course, because "Remember, honey, we're on a budget"). I threw in a Zebco 202 combo with hooks and split-shot all shrink-wrapped in plastic— exactly the same outfit I used to have back even before the days when I thought "culpability" was just another word for selling out.

So there we were one cool day in April, Gabe standing only half as tall as his fishing rod, on the banks of a little trout pond in Northport. I tried not to show it, but nothing in my entire angling life to that point equaled the immensity of that afternoon.

I wanted Gabe to enjoy his first fishing experience. I secretly prayed that his first cast would not only hurl the tiny minnow I had fixed to his hook far out into the middle of that wondrous black-water unknown but at the same time, would propel this little son of mine into a lifelong love of something his doting and simpleminded father holds third only to God and family. But I had prepared myself for just the opposite—that he might not like fishing at all. That was okay, too. I am determined not to be one of those prodding parents who try to turn their kids into something they're not.

Surely everyone who has a child can remember the first time they felt changed, the exact moment when they finally felt like an actual parent and that happiness—life—with all our goals, ambitions, and petty personal desires suddenly shifts. One day it hits you; all of a sudden, none of it matters.

Perhaps for the first time in your entire heady and self-absorbed life, you finally have a forehead-slapping epiphany that people really are deathly serious when they say they would give everything for their kids. The inkling might come with a gesture, a word, or an impulse that suggests all this time that maybe you're not just going numbly through the motions of what it means to sacrifice, but doing it out of some hidden instinct you maybe didn't even know you had.

I heard people talk of it happening the first time they feel the baby kicking or one day out of nowhere, just driving along, you hear a report come over the radio of yet another missing child and, thinking of your own, are struck with a very real and sickening sadness. I've always been slow on the uptake, hardheaded, fierce at defending my time, my personal wants and passions, not to mention being more than too boorishly cautious when it came to offering into others hands certain, damaged pieces of myself.

It probably sounds silly if you're not a fisherman, but the moment I really felt like a father happened not at Gabe's first steps, not when he smiled, or first called me "Daddy," but rather on the banks of that little mill pond when the bobber we were watching suddenly popped, shot down, and disappeared. I didn't even have my normal hog-headed impulse to seize the rod Gabe was fumbling with, set the hook, and simply play the fish to the bank myself. I let him take his time and do it all, giving whatever might happen next into his tiny hands.

Knotting Matters

This past New Year's Day we spent a snowy afternoon at a friend's place in the woods. A campfire was burning in the backyard and as darkness came and the party was winding down, people gathered outside to toss their resolutions into the flames. Everybody was standing around afterward fisting bottles of beer, stomping their boots in the snow, and chatting about how they were going to exercise more, quit smoking, lose some weight—the usual things. I vowed to finish writing my novel; get out of debt; spend more time with family and friends; and learn to tie some knots.

"The knot-thing," as my wife began to call it, seemingly came out of nowhere. For thirty-some years I've managed quite nicely, leading quite an active and outdoorsy life if I do say so, with a sum total of knot knowledge that pretty much boiled down to a handful of fishing knots and a few twisted variations of the venerable old "granny."

I had ratchet straps and bungee cords for lashing the canoe to the car top. Nylon cable-ties in an assortment of lengths, bright colors, and sizes. For everything else—duct tape. There wasn't a thing I couldn't hitch, bind, and fasten together with a couple rolls of that stuff.

So why knots? I might not have recognized it at the time, but I should have known: Everything in this life is connected. I kicked off the New Year with a book of camping knots that included six from the *Boy Scout Handbook*—the square knot, sheet bend, sheepshank, clove hitch, round turn and two half hitches, and bowline (pronounced *bow-lin*). I was astounded to discover that the world speed record for tying these six on individual ropes has stood since 1977. Just 8.1 seconds. I couldn't even tie just one of my "quadruple grannies" that fast.

With these six basic Boy Scout knots, a person could tie off, tie up or tie down any object or unwieldy load. Any normal person would have drawn a big smiley next to this one on his resolution list—mission accomplished.

But thirty days and thirty new knots later, I was still walking around with a hank of rope in my back pocket, practicing my knots at home and even out in public. To learn these new knots, I practiced with my eyes closed—the anglers loop, the figure eight, the three-part crown, the double constrictor, the fisherman's knot. I even practiced in bed with the lights off until one night, clicking on the lamp, "Look, honey, a hangman's noose!"

My wife lay on the pillow, pupils the size of birdshot, staring up cross-eyed at my latest creation dangling inches from her nose. I, meanwhile, reclined on an elbow next to her, recalling almost verbatim what I learned in my book that day.

"A real hangman's noose only has eight coils, not thirteen. That's a myth, you know. This knot can be used to tie on a fishing lure, to add a little mass to the end of a throwing line, or even to snare small game in a survival situation—"

"Bob," she cut me off. "You're starting to freak me out."

Nancy wasn't the only one who found my latest obsession with "knotology" to be somewhat pointless and more than a bit bizarre. When an editor for one of the biggest outdoor magazines in America called to see if I had any new article ideas, I proposed one on the outdoorsy importance of some basic knot know-how.

"People just don't know anything about knots anymore," I said.

"Hmmm. Yes," he replied. "Well, I just don't see most of our readers caring about that. I mean, c'mon, it's not like learning to tie a few knots is really going to change your life."

Ah, but tell that to the sorry sod who made international news recently after he tripped over his shoelaces—a basic bowknot failed—while touring the local Fitzwilliam Museum in Cambridge. After tumbling face-first into a display of three sixteenth-century Qing dynasty vases that crashed to the floor into literally a "million pieces," the man was reportedly still sitting there, shell-shocked, when museum staff appeared. Stunned witnesses watched as he kept pointing to his shoelace babbling, "There it is; that's the culprit!"

I loved the history of knots. "Knotologists," for example, believe the common square knot pre-dates the invention of the plow and the wheel. Cavemen snared game with snares tied with loop knots, and lashed their flint arrow and hatchet heads to wooden shafts using knots tied with plant fiber and animal gut. Ancient Romans and Greeks invented dozens of hitches and bends still used by seaman and fishermen today. The Chinese, before the advent of buttons and belts, tied decorative sinnet chain sashes and elaborate button knots. From sailors to surgeons, underground miners to astronauts, there are knots specific to every avocation and profession.

I love knots with names like "Turk's Head" and "Bimini Twist," "The Frustrator" and "Monkey Fist." Knots like "The Cat's Paw" and the "Alpine Butterfly" can be sensual in name, too.

There are trick knots like the "Tom Fool," the "Jumping," and "Go-Go" knot used by magicians. Knot people have their own corny jokes (*I'm not a blonde. I'm knot! I'm knot!*). There's a knot tier's guild, knotting conventions, and hundreds of books on knotting, including the bible of them all—*The Ashley Book of Knots*—Clifford Ashley's magnum opus finally completed and released in 1944, which includes roughly 4,000 knots that Ashley, an illustrator and seaman, discovered while touring the harbors and countries of the world.

Tying knots, I found, can be a therapeutic, too—an exercise like knitting or working a little jigsaw puzzle. It's perfect for occupying an anxious mind while sitting on an airplane bound for New York and, later, as you wait in some cold Manhattan office for the editor to come back from lunch only to say, "Gee, you know, on second thought, I don't think this is going to work for us." Or maybe, a week later, while you're sitting in your Jeep down some dirt road that dead ends in Lake Michigan where there's nothing between you and the blue abyss but a few tall trees—massive, gray beech trees with low, stout branches. There you are, with nothing but a bit of rope in your hands, idly trying to gauge how much weight one of those big old bastards might hold.

Some days you just can't help but feel hung up on the pointlessness of it all, as if you're coming undone. We all sometimes question what really matters. What's it all for anyway—the mind-numbing routine of daily living and work, work, working for nothing but a passenger's seat full of bills you can't pay, services you never asked for, and things you can't remember if you ever really wanted?

What are the ties that bind each of us to this life—to certain people, the land, family, or even, heaven help you, your job? And how strong are these connections, really, when just one careless wrap, tuck, or twist with the rope's working end can make the whole thing tangle or fall apart?

"When the body sinks into death," said Antoine de Saint, "the essence of a man is revealed. Man is a knot, a web, a mesh into which relationships are tied."

When you look at it that way, suddenly knots seem metaphoric. A knot tied is, after all, one of the few things in this life that is either completely right or wrong. For me, it makes sense to understand them, to learn by feel and memory how every one is tied. Then, in those dark moments—when you reach the end of your rope, to paraphrase Franklin Roosevelt—you not only have a knot to grab onto but, with luck, a tethered line and an anchor that will hold through any storm.

Tom

On any other stream, the damn fine work those beaver did seemingly overnight would have gone unnoticed save for certain birds and fish, four-footed animals, and, I suppose, some people drawn by the quiet refuge that still waters provide. But as it happened, that tiny trickle—a creek ordinarily so narrow a boy could swing over it Tarzan-style on the branches of any one of the weeping willows lining the ditch along Route 31—was backed up for a quarter mile, turning the parking lot of our town's only Bob's Big Boy into one big, happy duck pond.

The message on my machine said the restaurant's owner wanted the beavers out. Never mind why they called me. The point is, for better or worse, I took the dirty job. It paid by the head; my call on what to do with the catch, which is how I met Tom.

His place was farther out into this country than I'd ever ventured before—muddy Midwest farm country—not the kind of land the summertime tourists ever have a reason to go and see. Between there and here, the road signs are all in numbers (9 ROAD, 20 ROAD, for example) corresponding to every square mile of the flat, featureless farmland out there. Occasionally, every half-mile on the grid to be exact, a sign like the one for 29½ ROAD would appear. Such an odd name for a road, I began to wonder if these dusty lanes led to some parallel universe or far-out Twilight-Zone town after I passed one and saw standing underneath a man in bib-overalls and a Kromer hat working at the dirt with leaf rake. He wore a huge gold cross around his neck and, as I sped by, made a high holy gesture with his hand before flipping me the finger.

The road found the forest again where the signs had the usual names a mind is accustomed to wrapping around. Then came another sign: this one calling for a Libertarian president. Tom lived at the end of that muddy lane.

Here's a man that two hundred years ago, by virtue of his occupation, might have been one of the wealthiest in the North. A high roller in a black suit and stove pipe just like John Jacob Astor—this nation's first multimillionaire—who made his fortune in fur after opening the American Fur Company on Mackinaw Island in the early 1800s.

Now, *the* fur buyer for all of northern Michigan lives in a tilting trailer amidst a dozen or so junker cars up on blocks. A Newfoundland dog as big and black as a bear came to greet me, a deer leg bone hanging out both sides of its muzzle like a hoary handlebar mustache, weaving his way between an old washing machine and a couple rusty fifty-gallon drums.

I found Tom with a propane torch and small sledgehammer, lying under the rear end of a two-tone Bronco. He stared up into the undercarriage, perplexed, then *clang! clang! clang!* with the hammer followed by long gazes of bewilderment. I said "Hello," or something like it.

By way of a reply, he picked up the torch, cranked the blue flame on high, and said, "Hey, can you slide that gas tank over here?"

Right.

Inside the barn were the pelts of red and gray foxes, coyotes, otter, muskrats, and scores of raccoon all stretched over boards evenly spaced and hanging from the rafters in neat rows. Anyone not interested in such things might find the place having the charm of a slaughterhouse. I'm an occasional trapper and even I couldn't help but wonder what kind of dreams a man takes home after spending days, months—for Tom, the last thirty years—so long breathing air heavy with the odor of animal fat and blood.

I had never before seen a man work the hide off an animal like that. He wielded the knife with surgical cuts, so sparingly and with such care, that it somehow took all the gruesomeness out of the task. The fatty side of the skin when pulled back was clean and warm and white and without one drop of blood; when finally the beaver was totally undressed, its head was ribboned with red muscle and tendons. The eyes, like tiny round balls of obsidian, resembled something insectile.

Tom is a smallish man with stooped shoulders and the dark, whiskered face of a mountain man. I remember those oversized hands, a worker's hands, the big fingers greasy and shining with animal fat. He told me that one year when the raccoon were thick, for six weeks he skinned, fleshed, and hung up to dry the furs of at least one hundred every day.

I'm trying to remember some of the other things he told me; how, for example, everything hanging in that barn would be sold at auction come spring to buyers as far away as China and Russia, who then would ship the bundles home to garment makers for sewing into mittens and coats. Tacking the beaver blanket in a perfect circle on a board, he talked about the land, the weather, and the habits of furry predators. We talked of night creatures— coyotes and fox and bobcats—animals rarely seen even by most of those who now call this country home.

Listening to Tom, I found myself wondering what most of the people who now live up here would think of him, and me by implication of simply being here, and of this place in the woods where he works. For some, country is more than just a word to describe a popular trend in home décor. Real country is more than just a lifestyle that calls for wearing jeans, flannel shirts, and work boots more for fashion than for practicality's sake. I guess it's no surprise that some who look at country this way often miss the real thing when they see it. Or maybe what I mean to say is that we don't always look it in the eye because of the fact that country, real country, is not exactly pretty all the time.

My Michigan-ness

One of the drudgeries of writing for magazines for a living is that occasionally it makes good business sense to travel east to the city where the editors of most major publications in America drink their lunch. When you live up in Michigan—and it's a half-day's drive south and a $100 in gas just to cross over the state line—that means getting on a plane.

Now before you think this is just a setup to bash city living, I want to make clear that I'm not some boorish bumpkin who can't appreciate what towns and cities have to offer. If there were no places like New York—no towns at all—I'd be living in a mud hut. Life would be, as the philosopher Thomas Hobbes once famously said, solitary, poor, nasty, brutish, and short. My days would be spent really working, tending the garden, praying for rain, and gnawing on a bearskin until it was supple enough to sew up into a coat.

I've been lucky enough in my travels that I've experienced both city living and the closest thing to real wilderness in North America. For the record, my overall impression of the latter reminds me of a bit of trivia I once heard about none other than Thoreau. Upon laying eyes on really big, savage woods, Dear Henry once wrote how he beelined back to his Unabomber-style shack where, so shaken by the vast, unvarnished reality of the place, he holed up for weeks and resolved never to stray so far from his little golden pond again.

You might hear me complain about the traffic back east, but I'll never try to tell you that I'm so countrified that walking on asphalt all day hurts my feet. If nothing else, the first lesson we northern Michiganders learn is the value of always wearing sensible shoes.

I know, too, how to dress. I know you don't drive anywhere in winter up here without jumper cables, a tow chain, a sleeping bag, flares, and a shovel. Then there's the stuff I carry in my pockets. And that's where air travel comes in.

Living in northern Michigan and, to an extent, quitting a perfectly fine, blissfully mundane fulltime job to write for a living, has an overwhelming factor of unpredictability to it. It takes a certain mindset to call this place home—a ready-for-anything or call it a can-do-it-ness if you'd prefer. Being wired this way, I've found this has a material side, too. Nothing reminds me more of that when I'm forced to shed a little of my Michigan-ness to ride on a plane, especially in winter.

When traveling this time of year, it never escapes my notice that I'm perpetually way overdressed for the climate of my eventual destination. On the peg next to the door in my office hangs the same green wool bucket hat and like-colored Filson double-Mackinaw cruiser I got the year I moved up here.

Back when I traveled to New York almost once every quarter looking for work, every editor I met owned a black leather jacket and a matching pair of Doc Martins. Being more into function than fashion (and broke, need I mention yet again), I stuck with my rebel northwoodsman regalia, hoping my practical 45th-parallel style might carry with it to 45th Street; a Hunter S. Thompson meets Hemingway kind of vibe—writerly, rugged, maybe a bit eccentric.

(Note: Being a freelancer from northern fly-over country, which in Manhattan magazine offices is the writing equivalent of an out-of-town beggar holding a sign WILL WRITE FOR FOOD, my experience is that sometimes it pays to stand out even if they didn't exactly remember my name.)

I could put up with any joke or degree of sarcasm, provided it was wrapped around the promise of assignment, however small and remote.

"Nice coat. So what's it like up there in northern Michigan? Cold I bet. *Brrrrr!* Anyway, Bill, great ideas. Thanks for coming all this way. We'll try to find you something and give you call."

While my travel dress is the same, flying isn't anything like it was in the old days. I don't go east as much anymore, and it has nothing to do with a fear of militant Islamic whack-a-dos. Actually, statistically speaking, much more probable than a chance onboard encounter with some la-la jihadist packing C-4 in the soles of his hiking shoes is the very real threat that the plane you're riding in will plummet from the sky after smacking into a wedge of geese or sucking a turkey vulture into one of its turbo props. It's a fact.

It does bother me, however, that I used to be able to mosey onboard with the everyday contents of my pockets intact. On any given day that list includes—in addition to a wallet, some loose change, and a set of car keys—a pocketknife, a little P-38 can opener I keep on my key chain, and, even though I don't smoke, a butane lighter taken on after learning the hard way that, here in northern Michigan, you might bury your Toyota up to the hubs down some desolate snowbound wilderness two-track. In that situation, having a fire burning not only provides a little comforting light but also makes for a good hand-warming interlude between periodic fits of shoveling, cussing your bad luck, and hacking down bundles of alder whips to jam under a pair of spinning tires.

The pocketknife I've always carried, even back in the days when I fashioned myself a junior Jeremiah Johnson. For the record, you don't really realize how often a hank or rope and knife come in handy until you start carrying them. And what about the can opener? To explain that, all I can do is posit a reoccurring daydream that flashes in my head, triggered most often in flight by any sudden buckle of turbulence:

What if the plane you and I were riding went down, perhaps crashing on some desert island, and by some miracle we survived?

If you'd like a toasty fire come nightfall and had a hankering for a can of beans—heck, maybe even a real northern Michigan shore lunch served up special with fish I rounded up with a whittled stick fashioned into a trusty spear—I used to be your man.

I used to kick back cool and confident in flight wearing a Leatherman—a universally recognizable talisman of country-bumpkin everywhere—in a tiny black holster on my hip. Scissors, pliers, Phillips and flat head screwdrivers, a file, leather punch, and knife blade all in one—the ultimate in supercalifragilistic, way-cool multi-tools. I remember at least once coming to the rescue of an old lady in the aisle seat next to me after her reading glasses popped a lens on a flight from Chicago to JFK.

With a nod and tip of my goofy wool bucket hat—"All in a day's work, Ma'am."—I went from screwdriver to handy knife mode with a flick of the wrist and slowly quartered up the apple the flight attendant was passing out with my choice of chef's salad and chicken cordon bleu.

"Where you from, sonny?" the lady asked.

"Michigan," I said. "Northern Michigan.

"Ah. The country," she said with a nod, as if that somehow explained it all.

Sticks and Stones

The boy discovered the front yard this spring. Gabe is two and has been walking for months. Because we live in northern Michigan where winter lingers over such a great portion of any given year, this is the first spring where he's really been able to explore some of the tiny marvels long buried out there under a sea of snow.

Topping the list of fantastic new finds are pill bugs, pinecones, spiders, ants, and acorns. There's dirt and mud and—you're not going to believe this—sticks! Glorious sticks. He likes to pick them up and put them down. He carries, swings, and occasionally even eats them, twisting up his face and biting down much in a manner of a little fat man sampling a molar-busting piece of biscotti.

He started collecting sticks in his little red wheelbarrow—his "wee-bow"—and the dogs, two Labrador retrievers utterly mental about finding and fetching sticks themselves, began following him around like a pair of fawning Amazonian natives. They brought him sticks in the hopes that he might toss one, just once, dropping each offering at his toddling feet as if the boy were some sort of legendary god—The Great Keeper of The Sticks—or prodigal son, returned.

This went on for what felt like weeks, every day from dawn until the boy's nap at noon. He would sleep until three o'clock on the nose and then up again.

"Wee-bow-outside. Wee-bow-outside," he'd say.

April turned to May and springtime, with its southerly winds and warm rains nearly every night and day, meant the bountiful supply of sticks in the yard was without end. Every day we'd head outside to find the dewy grass covered with a new bumper crop. It was amazing! And, probably obvious by now, it was a little mind-bending how much time I sat around watching this.

But just as quickly as Gabe's stick fixation came, it passed; overnight, pebbles and rocks became the boy's new everything. One day, lumps of pinkish sandstone began to replace the rotting rods of aspen and gnarly hunks of pine and white birch cluttering the garage. There were discarded pieces of old cinder block and concrete, evidence of old construction, terracotta-colored hunks of old planting pots and some heavy hunks of limestone I had to help him dig up with a pick ax and a spade.

Most days, I just sat on the porch staring, profoundly perplexed, and literally surrounded by plastic milk crates and beach pails filled with these stones. I spent a lot of time thinking, that's for sure. I spent a lot of time wondering, *Is this it? Is this all there is?*

By the time he was thirty, George Custer was already a decorated war veteran, the commander of the 1st Michigan Calvary at Gettysburg. Ty Cobb was halfway into his legendary 22-year career with the Detroit Tigers. Thomas Edison invented the phonograph. Joe Louis was the heavyweight champion of the world. Ernest Hemingway had written *The Sun Also Rises* and *A Farewell to Arms*.

Spring was almost over, I was pushing thirty-five, and all I kept thinking about was how many more springtimes I had left to land a 20-inch brown trout on a fly. And what about *my* work? At this point, would I ever write anything worthwhile if hadn't done so already?

One of the insidious mental tortures that came with staying at home with a toddler, my son, was the mundane toil and everyday routine…the think, think, thinking all the time about everything to do and everything left undone.

New parents only ever talk about this stuff in therapy because you're seen as nothing but a festering, open sore of a subhuman if you're not anything but always swooning that your little one was born in the first place, born with all his fingers and toes.

Part of me just couldn't stop dwelling on a thousand other things I'd rather be doing at any given moment. At the same time, I felt torn and confused by the underlying knowledge that there was no better way to spend my time, no place in the world I'd rather be.

This left me feeling wretched and self-loathing most of the time. How undeserving a soul was mine that I could even think about fishing or work instead of just being with my son?

Elbows on my knees, chin resting in my hands, I just sat, letting the stones pile up around me until one day my mind finally came back into focus. My eyes settled on the boy sitting alone in the grass, way out there in the yard, idly stacking some of the stones he'd found that day.

That's when I saw it, when I picked myself up and joined him. We built a tiny stone tower, a cairn, together right there in the grass. After that, we built another, the next one even larger than the first. Stacking one stone on top of another, I began to see metaphor in the careful balancing act of it all. I felt the weight on my own shoulders lifting as the rocks fit and piled upward. And I thought, *What is life anyway but right here?* Isn't life, after all, just an act of balancing and re-balancing random burdens, obligations, and gifts—everything—that comes in realizing a dream and of living, life, in a place divine?

River Notes

Three Days of the Savage Life

I'm all by myself in this canoe, maybe on this whole river, given the time of year and the fact that for days they've been calling for one hell of a storm.

Snow. There's over a foot on the ground already, which makes it great for spotting deer. Shortly after the put-in this morning, I drifted by a pair of them—two does—bedded down under a cedar tree a stone's throw from the water's edge. For a moment, I considered my bow, lying there unstrung in the front. Then I thought better of it; the deer were too close, too soon. I paddled past without looking at them, without looking directly into their eyes, and they let me by without bolting, without so much as twitching an ear.

I'm remembering now the color of their fur—a soft gray, like soot, almost as gray as the sky that weighs down so heavy now…

Anchored in a quiet backwater slough where the Boardman River flows into Brown Bridge Pond…

A moment ago, there were mallards here—five drakes and a hen—that shot up over the trees and circled twice before flying out high over the lake.

Ducks are fair game on this float, and had these given me the opportunity I would not have been as disinterested in arrowing one

143

as I had been with the deer. The only food in my canoe is a three-pound bag of potatoes and three cans of tuna fish. A spartan diet; one I hope to supplement with some freshly killed meat before long.

Trout fishing here earlier this summer, it seemed as if I was constantly walking up on deer bedded down on the riverbank. Of course, this got me thinking about swapping my fly rod for a bow come autumn. But the plan got pushed back until now, during what looks like winter.

Certainly, there are wilder rivers in northern Michigan—more secluded waters to hunt and lose oneself for a while. I fished much of the Boardman this summer, so I know the meandering course that river makes. Scattered along the upper reaches are cottages and summer homes, while the lower part is usually choked with canoers and beer-swilling inner-tubers in summertime. But all of them are gone now, thanks to the cold, gray promise of snow.

As for the river—truth is, even an inexperienced paddler could float the length of the Boardman in a day. But I'm hunting, so I plan to stretch that a little. In *A Witchery of Archery*, Maurice Thompson wrote of "Three Weeks of the Savage Life." I have less than three days…

After dragging the canoe ashore, I pulled it under the boughs of a cedar tree. There I cleared away a place to sleep: a shallow bed in the snow dug down into the leaves, down into the bare, black earth. I laid out a ground cover (a blue tarp folded in half), my sleeping pad, cold-weather bag, and the rest of my gear. The canoe placed over the top formed a perfect makeshift bivouac.

I hunted the hill up behind camp for nearly two hours, then made my way back toward the river. My bow, a 64-inch hickory selfbow, is one of the first bows I ever made so it's kind of clumsy and heavy looking. Selfbows can be particular in inclement weather—specifically the rain—but this one has never given me a lick of trouble. I've killed with it before, so I have that much-needed air of confidence.

144

The snow was soft and made for quiet walking. Instead of deer, all I crept up on were squirrels. Three grays and a black. I took a shot at the black squirrel where he sat on fallen log. It was a hurried shot and I missed, then spent the better part of a half hour digging for my arrow lost in the snow.

It started snowing soon after that, a fine, heavy snow. There was no wind, just the snowflakes wafting down like a million tiny moths, so beautiful that I decided to sit and watch it pile up for awhile before heading back to camp.

I cut down the hill toward the sound of the river, peeling a little bark from every birch tree I passed. Bark from white birch makes a good fire starter. It lights even when wet. It wasn't long before my pockets were bulging with the stuff, and it pleased me beyond measure to be thinking of such necessary things…

From deer to rabbits: I found tracks of both down in the alders and Juneberry bushes along the river. Having already resigned myself to a dinner of tuna fish and boiled potatoes, I didn't hold much hope of spotting either. Then I heard the ducks chattering out on the water, back in the slough I had chased them from a couple of hours before. The snow was still coming down, now falling as fine as dust. Everything was so crisp, clear, and cold. It sounded as if the ducks were right there, just around the next bend.

Creeping closer, I found them some distance away—surely the same ducks that had been here earlier in the afternoon. The drakes were tipping over one another to get their fill of whatever was down below. I sat hunkered down behind a drift of snow, watching until it was clear they didn't intend to come closer.

It was a long shot, but a makeable one. In less time than it takes to write it, I picked out a drake in the middle of the paddling and let go an arrow. By the time it got there, another duck had climbed over the back of the one I wanted. At first, it appeared as if I had missed all of them. Up and away I watched them, not quite believing that I had missed. As it turned out, I hadn't.

One of them faltered, went limp, and fell just before they cleared the trees. It splashed down on the edge of the slough and I set off running along the bank to intercept him. The drake was a beautiful greenhead. The killing shot was a small gash on his neck where the broadhead passed an inch or so under the bill.

After that, I felt damn near invincible walking back to camp. I tried to take in everything: the soul-quieting snow; the heft of the mallard in my hand; the wood rattle of my arrows in the quiver as I walked. Everything. All the while knowing it might be quite some time until I felt this way again.

After plucking the duck clean (the breast skin the color of autumn corn), I found my little hideout under the boughs of the cedar tree and built a fire with the birchbark I had collected. The flames I fed with snow-covered limbs that hissed and popped. The duck cooked at a miserably slow pace, only to come out a little dry—and a little burned, too—when it was done. In spite of that, it tasted as good as any duck I've ever eaten.

It's dark outside as I remember all this to paper. I put a candle lantern up on the underside of the canoe seat, and I'm lying here now, barely able to see the page under its dull glow, packed in by a down sleeping bag. My quarters are tight, though wonderfully comfortable. For warmth, I wrapped a stone from the fire ring in a towel and stuffed it down into the foot of my bag. Before going to sleep, I will look outside just to make sure it hasn't stopped snowing.

I hope it snows all night. I hope to be covered over with the stuff by morning.

Saturday, November 22

Cold this morning and wakened every couple of minutes or so because of it. In spite of that, I felt strangely refreshed—alive—when I rose from my snow-covered tomb.

The sun was just coming over the trees, but it was miserable cold out in the air. A cup of coffee would have tasted fine, but I hadn't had the foresight to bring any. So I settled for a cup of river water, which was so chilly going down it made my throat ache.

The snow stopped sometime during the night, but so much of it had fallen that a passerby would never have noticed my camp. Even the fire pit was covered over; my tracks all but obliterated.

While getting my gear together, I ate a couple of handfuls of granola from the bag I had ferreted away in my pack. Then I set off across the slough to retrieve the arrow that had killed the duck for me last evening.

The sky this morning was powder blue and streaked with clouds the color of fire. All the trees along the banks were bent over, their branches hanging down, laden with snow that everywhere glowed with a soft pink light. The arrow stuck in the riverbank, only its fletching showing. I pulled it free and paddled in close to shore, paddling slowly, languidly, watching for deer, for squirrels— anything that I might arrow for lunch later that afternoon.

The Boardman River below the Brown Bridge impoundment runs faster than above, almost too fast for hunting. Past the first bend, I surprised another paddling of mallards…twenty-five, fifty… too many to even begin to count. They all lifted up from the water, a literal wall of mallards, and were gone so fast I didn't even try to reach for my bow.

I drifted tight to the shoreline, veering away only when a log or fallen tree—a "sweeper"—got in the way, spooking the tiny trout that darted under the boat and disappeared in the black water midstream.

Not long after the ducks, I came upon the mouth of Swainson Creek and what remains of the old bridge. "October 1907" is etched upon one of the crumbling cement trusses.

The bridge seemed a good place to stop and hunt for a while. I fished here this summer and had twice walked up on deer bedded down in the red diamond willow and switch alders.

The wind this morning was perfect, blowing right out of the north. So after stringing my bow, I slipped on my waders and started still-hunting my way along the riverbank.

The gurgle of the river made for quiet walking, and the snow was piled so high on the banks it was like peering over a wall to see if anything was hidden on the other side.

I hadn't gone far before spotting a deer, a doe, deep in the alders. I saw her ears first, then the soft curl of her back. She was close and looking away, but in too tricky a spot to manage a shot. One step on the bank and the snow packed down underfoot sounded exactly like it does when you sit in a leather chair. She sprang to her feet and bolted. Then more deer appeared, flashes of them, making off ahead of me through the alders like rabbits. Looks like I'll be eating a can of tuna fish before shoving off again…and maybe a potato, which I'll wash in the river and eat raw.

A grouse! A big gray one. Rounding a bend I saw it just glide across the river—so close I could see its black, beady eye—then set down right inside the trees on the riverbank close to shore. I dropped anchor, taking one arrow from my quiver—one shot—knowing I probably wouldn't get even that.

It landed on the other side of a sweeper—a big fallen maple that looked as if lightning had blasted its middle into toothpicks. The entire crown of the tree was hanging in the water and made for a perfect bit of cover to sneak up behind.

But this grouse was a wary one. He went up and out of there like a clap of thunder without me ever getting so much as a glimpse of him.

I crawled up on the bank and found where he had been sitting in the snow. When I knelt to get a closer look at the track, another grouse flushed from a deadfall to my left. I got a good long look at this one, perhaps too long, as another grouse flushed from the same spot. Expecting more, I looked for another grouse in that tangle—trying to separate brush from bird—staring as hard as I have ever looked at anything. When I was positive they had all gone, I took a step and another shot out.

I paddled hard through a long stretch where it seemed as if around every bend was one vacated summer home after another. But the river would again find its way back into the woods, and once there, under the cool of the cedars, the snow-covered hills rose up from the water from either shore.

The rest of the afternoon I spent still-hunting the top of a ridge, finding only the old tracks of deer, trails leading down toward the river, into a bowl-shaped hollow dark with cedar and white pine.

Tuna fish and boiled potatoes for dinner. And a restless night in the cold, wakened regularly by thumps on the canoe from snow pack falling from the branches above.

SUNDAY, NOVEMBER 23

The deer you see while float-hunting are usually bedded down. Sometimes they are sleeping, which to me is one of the most unnatural things to behold in the world. Human hunters just aren't supposed to *see* things like that.

Stalking along the river, I once crept upon a deer kicking and twitching in its dreams like a dog. This morning, the one I find is cloaked in hoarfrost. Still as stone. Even as I sit here writing it, looking at what's left of her sprawled in the canoe at my feet, it seems impossible, as if the past couple of days have culminated in a dream.

When I woke this morning, I had been in fact dreaming of the days before. Dreaming of what's real. I never understood that feeling of being outside oneself until this morning, waking from that dream and then packing, getting back in the canoe, and paddling alone and surrounded in that eerie snowy silence...everything exactly the same as it was in sleep.

Three days within earshot of a river and suddenly to hear the gurgling rush of the current, I really have to listen, as if it were the pulse of my own heart or the sound of blood coursing through my veins. Suddenly, what has come to me is a feeling of belonging to this world, an idea most every hunter entertains: a sense that we could make it out here if we wanted to…if everything else went bad and we *needed* to.

The doe had dug out a place for herself in the fork of a fallen, snow-covered tree. I first thought her a stump. Then the image took shape. A deer! Drifting past, I anchored the canoe downriver and stalked back against the current.

I watched her dozing for a moment, waiting for the wind to carry my scent toward her. She didn't leap to her feet, but instead rose like a tired old cow. The arrow skimmed over the snow bank between us, and when it passed through her chest, a tiny cloud of white air puffed from the hole.

With that, the spell was broken. I followed crimson splotches of her blood in the snow and found her a short distance later, where she had fallen in the cattails along an oxbow frozen over. She dragged easily back over the snow. Now as I remember it to paper, I feel an urgency to be gone from here, a sudden revelation coming as quickly as the feeling of belonging, that I am not the savage this story suggests or that I often like to pretend.

I'm thinking of my wife waiting at the railroad bridge downriver and how good it will be to see her and the boy. How good it will be to shed these boots and layers of wool, to just sit with her and him in our warm house with the air smelling of orange peels and cinnamon sticks simmering in a pot on the stove. Three days, though it suddenly feels as if I've been away forever.

Pushing away from the bank, I dig the paddle deep, letting the river take hold of the living and the dead, pulling away on a strong current leading me home.

Praise for...

Beast of Never, Cat of God: The search for the eastern puma

(The Lyons Press, 2005)

Voted a "Notable Book" by the Library of Michigan in 2006

"...a wonderfully engaging book on the cougar controversy and the pathetically warring factions of believers and cynics who demand a level of proof rarely available to criminal prosecutors."
—Jim Harrison, author of *True North*

"Here is a book that should be required reading for everyone who is or will become a state, federal or provincial wildlife agency employee..."
—Wildlife Management Institute, *Outdoor News Bulletin*

"*Beast of Never, Cat of God* is a curiously unique detective story, a probing investigation peopled with edgy characters—the most candid, sometimes savage, taxonomy of human/puma aficionados ever assembled. You won't forget these characters or the great cats that yet prowl the shadows of our most primordial dreams."
—Doug Peacock, author of *Grizzly Years*

"...a riveting and wondrous book..." —*The Flint Journal*

"With *Beast of Never, Cat of God*, Bob Butz nails the mystery and longing for something wild and primordial that lurks in all of us. Both funny and haunting, *Beast of Never, Cat of God* is the rarest of reads—a meditation cloaked as a real page-turner." —Elwood Reid, screenplay writer and author of *If I Don't Six*

"…a fine piece of wildlife journalism that should interest many readers, especially those who want to read about how politics, money, and wildlife science can affect the search for a mysterious animal…"
—*North American BioFortean Review*

"This is a journey into wilderness and the imagination as serendipitous as *The Orchid Thief*. Butz's lyricism is matched by his relentless honesty, giving a taut portrait of vivid sinew and rich heart, a beast whose shadows cut across our lives in ways we don't always understand. Butz's soul searching and naturalist's vivid grasp, tooth and nail, breathe the beast to life." —Doug Stanton, author of *In Harm's Way*

"The eastern mountain lion haunts our domesticated dreams, infusing our too-tame world with hope and excitement. In *Beast of Never, Cat of God*, Bob Butz follows this ghost cat through the woods of Michigan and the thickets of science, politics and the human heart, wrestling with his own skepticism and a belief that the great predator is still out there. Just like the enigmatic animal at its core, *Beast of Never, Cat of God*, holds and does not let go."
—Scott Weidensaul, author of *The Ghost with Trebling Wings: Science, Wishful Thinking and the Search for Lost Species*

"…a fascinating report…" —*Grand Rapids Press*

"It is a fascinating story, and Butz tells it well." —*Wichita Falls Times Record News*